*The*

# COACH
# APPROACH

*to*

## SCHOOL LEADERSHIP

# Praise for *The Coach Approach to School Leadership*

*The Coach Approach to School Leadership* will change the conversation about how principals can serve as instructional leaders. Providing principals with tools and strategies to "put on their coach's hat" is a much-needed step for teaching and learning in our schools. So often, principals wonder how to provide relevant support to teachers, and serving as a principal-coach is a way to do just that. The authors' breadth of knowledge around both leadership and coaching makes this book a must-read for principals.

—Diane Sweeney, author of *Student-Centered Coaching: The Moves*

Among the most significant actions great principals do differently is getting out of the office and into classrooms to help teachers improve their skills. The authors of *The Coach Approach to School Leadership* present both a mindset and practical tools supporting school leaders to address the paradox of being both coach and supervisor. Through a focus on instructional coaching techniques and a deep understanding of the many challenges facing principals, this book offers extremely valuable guidance in the vital work of leading teachers to higher levels of effectiveness.

—Todd Whitaker, professor, speaker, and author of *What Great Principals Do Differently*

*The Coach Approach to School Leadership* is a must-read for all administrators who have been searching for a framework to help them move beyond the traditional practices of supervision and evaluation of teachers to the roles of learner and coach. Johnson, Leibowitz, and Perret not only provide specific resources and strategies to help you build your capacity, but also challenge you to reflect on the positive impact that effective coaching techniques can have on your overall school culture. This is a book that I will keep close by and continue to refer to time and time again.

—Jimmy Casas, author, speaker, and senior fellow, International Center for Leadership in Education

## ASCD MEMBER BOOK

Many ASCD members received this book as a
member benefit upon its initial release.

Learn more at: **www.ascd.org/memberbooks**

# The
# COACH
# APPROACH
## to
# SCHOOL LEADERSHIP

*Leading Teachers to
Higher Levels of Effectiveness*

JESSICA JOHNSON • SHIRA LEIBOWITZ • KATHY PERRET

Alexandria, Virginia USA

1703 N. Beauregard St. • Alexandria, VA 22311-1714 USA
Phone: 800-933-2723 or 703-578-9600 • Fax: 703-575-5400
Website: www.ascd.org • E-mail: member@ascd.org
Author guidelines: www.ascd.org/write

Deborah S. Delisle, *Executive Director;* Robert D. Clouse, *Managing Director, Digital Content & Publications;* Stefani Roth, *Publisher;* Genny Ostertag, *Director, Content Acquisitions;* Susan Hills, *Acquisitions Editor;* Julie Houtz, *Director, Book Editing & Production;* Miriam Calderone, *Editor;* Thomas Lytle, *Senior Graphic Designer;* Mike Kalyan, *Director, Production Services;* Keith Demmons, *Production Designer;* Kyle Steichen, *Senior Production Specialist*

All web links in this book are correct as of the publication date below but may have become inactive or otherwise modified since that time. If you notice a deactivated or changed link, please e-mail books@ascd.org with the words "Link Update" in the subject line. In your message, please specify the web link, the book title, and the page number on which the link appears.

PAPERBACK ISBN: 978-1-4166-2385-4    ASCD product #117025
PDF E-BOOK ISBN: 978-1-4166-2387-8; see Books in Print for other formats.

Quantity discounts are available: e-mail programteam@ascd.org or call 800-933-2723, ext. 5773, or 703-575-5773. For desk copies, go to www.ascd.org/deskcopy.

ASCD Member Book No. FY17-7 (May 2017, P). ASCD Member Books mail to Premium (P), Select (S), and Institutional Plus (I+) members on this schedule: Jan, PSI+; Feb, P; Apr, PSI+; May, P; Jul, PSI+; Aug, P; Sep, PSI+; Nov, PSI+; Dec, P. For current details on membership, see www.ascd.org/membership.

**Library of Congress Cataloging-in-Publication Data**

Names: Johnson, Jessica (Public school principal), author.
Title: The coach approach to school leadership : leading teachers to higher
   levels of effectiveness / Jessica Johnson, Shira Leibowitz, and Kathy
   Perret.
Description: Alexandria, Virginia : ASCD, [2017] | Includes bibliographical
   references and index.
Identifiers: LCCN 2017005076 (print) | LCCN 2017018392 (ebook) | ISBN
   9781416623878 (PDF) | ISBN 9781416623854 (pbk.)
Subjects: LCSH: School management and organization. | Teacher-principal
   relationships. | Teachers--In-service training. | School improvement
   programs.
Classification: LCC LB2805 (ebook) | LCC LB2805 .J645 2017 (print) | DDC
   371.2/012--dc23
LC record available at https://lccn.loc.gov/2017005076

*To the teachers, instructional coaches, and principals,*
*to the education thought leaders and authors,*
*and especially to our students, past and present,*
*with whom we have been privileged to be both vulnerable and curious,*
*discovering together the best within one another.*

*To our family, friends, and beloved writing buddy dogs*
*who have offered us encouragement and laughter*
*and kept us grounded while enabling us to grow, to learn, and to create.*

*And to our #educoach tribe: the participants in our weekly Twitter chat,*
*where our collaboration began and where we continue to gain*
*insight and inspiration.*

# The COACH APPROACH to SCHOOL LEADERSHIP

# Introduction

This book is the product of a journey embarked upon by three educators separated by geography and diverse experiences, but connected by a commitment to coaching as a means of improving our own practice and the quality of teaching and learning in our schools.

The three of us "met" on Twitter during the spring of 2011 through our shared interest in how school leaders might incorporate the approaches of instructional coaches to support professional learning for teachers. We created and have co-moderated #educoach, a weekly Twitter chat, ever since, developing a friendship unlike any other we have ever experienced. Through the years, without actually meeting in person, we have communicated weekly, preparing for and participating in this chat. Beyond our chat, we have coached one another through numerous career challenges and aspirations.

Although we are all educators, our experiences are quite different. Jessica is a public school principal in rural Wisconsin. Shira is an independent school principal who has served in suburban and urban schools in the greater New York City area. Kathy is an education consultant focusing on instructional coaching, literacy, and English learners who works with educators in many different schools throughout Iowa and across the United States. We all believe in the importance of coaching and being coached as educators, learners, and leaders.

As we engaged in meaningful conversation (albeit in 140 characters or less), we recognized that the substance of our weekly Twitter chats was helping us stretch ourselves as educators and leaders. We felt a book emerging through our conversations. It is a book that has been written gradually, over the course of several years. The slow development of this book is not only the result of the busy lives we lead and our difficulty dedicating time to write, but also the result of developing ideas through global conversations with educators via social media and in conversations with educators within our own schools. We invite you to engage with us and stretch yourself as an educator, a learner, and a leader and to help those around you to stretch themselves as well.

## What's in This Book?

When principals function primarily as learning leaders, the influence on the quality of learning in our schools is profound. Yet the pressure for school leaders to focus on evaluation and management rather than learning is tremendous. This book is for principals and other school or district leaders who want to lead teachers to higher levels of effectiveness and incorporate the principles of instructional coaching as a necessary part of serious school improvement.

In Chapter 1, we reframe the role of the principal, discussing the continuum of roles from judge to team captain to coach, and ultimately land on the importance of the coach role. Although a school leader could never fully play the role of an instructional coach, we delve into what it means to wear a coach's hat as a learning leader and explore how to make the shift from primarily being an evaluator, a supervisor, and a manager to being a learning leader using coaching techniques.

In Chapter 2, we show you what it looks like to put on your coach's hat by sharing what principal-coaches do each day as the learning leaders of their school. We challenge you to expand your classroom visits beyond the minimum requirements of your evaluation process and provide you with guidance to combine coaching with evaluation requirements.

In Chapter 3, we examine the most critical elements at the heart of every school: the relationships and culture. We ask you to reflect on yourself as a leader and how your staff perceive you. We dig into the partnerships that are essential to create in order to lead with a coach's hat.

In Chapter 4, we address feedback, the necessary component to support our teachers to grow professionally and improve the student learning in each classroom.

Leaders cannot effectively get into classrooms or spend time in coaching conversations with teachers if they cannot manage their time and workload effectively. For this reason, we provide you with strategies and resources that we have found to be effective for managing time—our most precious resource—in Chapter 5.

Finally, in Chapter 6, we invite you to consider ways to empower teachers to take ownership of their professional learning and support them to work together as a team.

Throughout the book, we provide a variety of vignettes from practitioners' perspectives, because so much of our growth has stemmed from learning from others' experiences and accomplishments. Teachers often say that they didn't learn what they needed to learn in their college coursework; it was actually teaching in a classroom that they learned how to teach. The same is true for school leadership. Our work is complex and challenging, and we have learned both from success and from missteps. In the process, we have been fortunate to develop a robust professional learning network (PLN) via social media and have connected with many school leaders, instructional coaches, and teachers, learning together and benefitting from one another's wisdom and firsthand experiences. The names used in this book are pseudonyms, but all of the vignettes are based on our own experiences or on stories we have heard from colleagues in our PLN. We are grateful for our colleagues' honesty and generosity in sharing their learned wisdom throughout this book.

We have made some of this book's tools available as blank forms for you to use in your own practice. You can access these resources in the Appendix and at http://www.ascd.org/ASCD/pdf/books/CoachApproach 2017forms.pdf. Use the password "CoachApproach117025" to unlock the PDF. In addition, at the end of each chapter, we ask you to reflect on your current reality and provide actionable next steps to help you move forward in your practice.

As you read, we encourage you to reach out and connect with us or our PLN on Twitter via the hashtags #educoach and #coachapproach. If you have not yet discovered the power of a PLN on Twitter, then you are in for a great deal of rich learning and insight from and with others in the field.

# One

# Hero Maker: Reframing the Principal's Role

"You are heroes," a uniformed police officer told a group of teachers, who reacted with a spontaneous round of applause. He was leading a lockdown drill, helping teachers practice how to respond if there were an intruder in the school or its vicinity. The officer began his presentation not by telling teachers what to do or how brave they would need to be, but by paying tribute to the consistent, quiet courage teachers already show day in and day out. He acknowledged that although the prospect of keeping company with unsavory characters at 3:00 a.m. did not faze him, he would be terrified to spend his days in a room filled with children.

Teachers are *heroes*.

Principals, along with other school leaders, are *hero makers*.

Roland Barth, founder of the Principals' Center at the Harvard Graduate School of Education, is quoted as having said, "The best principals are not heroes—they are hero-makers." For us, this humble eschewing of the title of hero in favor of a supporting role is the essence of principal-coaching. Our own journeys, along with those of many other school leaders, instructional coaches, and teachers with whom we have been privileged to learn, have convinced us that fostering a school culture of instructional coaching is a potent pathway to improving the quality of learning and community in our schools. That culture begins with the principal.

Although central to school improvement efforts, the role of principal-coach is infused with paradox. Typically, instructional coaches do not have supervisory responsibilities. They are committed to supporting teacher learning using a range of approaches, including planning one-on-one with teachers, modeling, observing, and offering targeted feedback or training to teachers in their classrooms. Because instructional coaches do not evaluate, they can encourage risk taking while ensuring safety. They can support teachers through challenging times with the promise of confidentiality. By contrast, principals, ultimately accountable for the quality of learning in their schools, must set high professional expectations, evaluate teacher effectiveness, make budgetary decisions, allocate resources, assign teachers to classes, and, at times, determine whether or not to rehire a teacher.

Principals and teachers alike may wonder, *How can principals possibly coach when they must evaluate? How can teachers feel safe to experiment, take risks, and reveal vulnerabilities with a person who makes important decisions about their employment?* To reconcile the apparently contradictory roles of supervisor and coach, leaders must

1. Reframe the role of the principal.
2. Nurture a schoolwide culture of coaching and professional collaboration.
3. Acknowledge the vulnerability inherent in professional learning.

## Reframing the Role of the Principal

Let's consider a sports metaphor: if a school were a team, what would the principal be? Judge? Captain? Coach? Manager? Owner? Sportscaster? Physical therapist? Cheerleader? Groundskeeper? Promoter? Fan?

You could probably make an argument for any of these roles. The way we envision the varying roles of principals is as a continuum, with judge at one end and team captain at the other (see Figure 1.1). Toward the middle of the continuum stand principals who function primarily as coaches, supporting teachers' professional learning and navigating both the resulting vulnerability and the celebratory exploration integral to meaningful growth. The journey to becoming a principal-coach has the potential to transform learning for teachers in profound ways, resulting in immeasurable benefits for students. To understand the journey, it is important to consider the three main leadership approaches ranging along the continuum.

Figure 1.1

## The Continuum of Principals' Roles

JUDGE                              TEAM CAPTAIN

## Judges

Principals who behave primarily as judges tend to take formal district teacher evaluation protocols seriously, striving to assess teacher effectiveness using a range of technical measurements. These principals focus on high expectations. Like the silent judges in boxing and gymnastics matches, holding up a score without explanation, principal judges rely on their evaluative tools.

This style of principal leadership is expected in many schools, but it comes with risks. Functioning primarily as judge and evaluator, even with kindness and respect, can result in a negative school culture and an unexpected decrease in school quality. Yet those who resist the role of formal evaluator run the risk of being perceived as neglecting district expectations —a potentially treacherous position for a leader.

So what is a well-intentioned, capable principal to do?

There are ways to move away from functioning primarily as a judge and toward making the evaluation process an opportunity for reflection and learning. Doing so will require leaders to find new ways to fulfill mandated procedures while either weaving them into a more reflective process or coordinating a parallel process of supportive feedback for growth. With the approval of district supervisors and leaders, the principal can accomplish such a shift, in the process delighting teachers and leading to transformative trust building and meaningful school improvement.

## Team Captains

Principals who behave primarily as team captains tend to take teachers' unions seriously and strive to be advocates for teachers. Like affable peer leaders of sports teams, functioning as first among equals, principal team captains typically rely on charisma and connection. They tend to be quite popular with teachers.

Yet the team captain style of leadership also comes with risks. Embracing a comfortable camaraderie can lead to complacency, potentially stifling innovation and leading to a culture of mediocrity in which students do not receive the quality learning experiences they deserve.

Again, what is a well-intentioned, capable principal to do?

There are ways to move away from functioning primarily as a genial team captain and toward nudging teachers to seek out the joy and discomfort inherent in meaningful growth. With careful pacing, explanation, encouragement, and reassurance, principals can help teachers engage in the sometimes disconcerting yet ultimately invigorating process of reflective, substantive professional learning.

## Coaches

At the middle of the continuum are principals who behave primarily as coaches, carefully balancing high expectations with robust supports. Principal-coaches see their role as learning leaders, directing resources to those areas that are most likely to affect the quality of student learning. These leaders visit classrooms and offer nonjudgmental feedback to teachers, provide time and training for teachers to work collaboratively on enhancing student learning, and creatively allocate resources in order to provide teachers with high-quality instructional coaching. Without neglecting their evaluative role, they transform formal evaluation processes into opportunities for engaged professional reflection and learning. While holding high expectations, principal-coaches support teachers as professionals and care about them as individuals.

Although shifting to a principal-coaching model has a significant positive effect on teaching and learning, it does come with some risks. District leaders may remain committed to more formal evaluative procedures. Teachers who have received exemplary or even satisfactory evaluations from leaders using the principal-judge approach may resist increasing their effort in professional learning, as a serious coaching model demands. Alternatively, teachers who have worked with principal team captains may find new expectations, even offered with support, a harsh imposition. Regardless of the prior leadership model, at least some teachers who have not experienced coaching will likely express skepticism about its benefits. They may also worry that the principal is recommending coaching because of low satisfaction with their performance rather than offering it as a gift that all professionals deserve.

So yet again, what is a well-intentioned, capable principal to do?

Although there is no recipe for transforming one's leadership style, principals can begin to reframe their role through careful and ongoing collaboration with both supervisors and teachers and a commitment to learning a number of new coaching approaches. The results can be transformative, unleashing teachers' potential and inspiring a culture of joyous curiosity about what's possible for each teacher and student.

It's true that because of their evaluative role, principals can never fully embody the role of coach. Finding balance on the continuum between judge and team captain requires ongoing navigation and adjustment. Still, although the task is challenging, we believe that supporting teachers' professional growth is the most effective way to improve the quality of our schools.

Principals wear many "hats." Throughout this book, we refer deliberately to "the coach's hat" and "the evaluator's hat." Because we firmly believe that building on teachers' strengths and helping them gain skill in areas of weakness are among the most powerful roles of a principal, our coach's hat remains our default hat—the leadership stance we use most of the time with most of our teachers. In difficult cases when we are concerned with a teacher's performance, we explain that we are speaking as a supervisor, with our evaluator's hat on, and make our expectations clear. The time to switch hats isn't always immediately obvious; we may see ineffective teaching practices that we believe will improve but instead deteriorate. At whatever point we determine coaching is no longer enough and feel deeply concerned about a teacher's performance, we must be honest with the teacher. In addition to making expectations clear, it is our responsibility to put alternative supports in place to help the teacher meet expectations. If the teacher does not improve, we owe it to our students to decide whether he or she should be retained.

Still, we see no reason to let the small number of difficult situations affect our decision to function as coach for the majority of the time, focusing on supervision for professional growth rather than judgmental evaluation.

# Nurturing a Schoolwide Culture of Coaching and Professional Collaboration

Among our favorite leadership quotes is the following, often attributed to John Quincy Adams: "If your actions inspire others to dream more, learn more, do more, and become more, you are a leader." We might tweak this quote just a bit to read, "If your actions inspire others to dream more, learn more, do more, and become more, you are a *teacher.*" Leading and teaching are not so different, after all.

We believe that coaching and professional collaboration form the link that connects great leadership, great teaching, and great learning. Thus, an essential component of principal-coaching is creating a schoolwide culture of coaching and professional collaboration. This culture involves not merely action but also interaction, not merely learning but also relationship. It stretches far beyond any one person, including the principal. Depending on the school, the central participants may include superintendents and other district leaders, assistant principals, curriculum leaders, psychologists or guidance counselors, department chairs, and teacher leaders. Ultimately, in successful cultural transformations, a majority of teachers become actively involved in crafting professional learning experiences and take ownership of their own learning.

To nurture such a culture, principals can adjust budgets to add coaching positions, reframe existing job descriptions to include some coaching components, demonstrate their appreciation for coaching, respect the confidentiality of coaches and teachers, and make clear that coaching is not remedial but a significant means of activating professional learning. Putting together a team of coaches and educational leaders who use coaching techniques is a creative process, with multiple possibilities even in budget-strapped schools. Are there specialists such as librarians, educational technology coordinators, or special education teachers whose schedules could include time for coaching? Are there teachers with expertise in particular subjects who could teach a lighter load and devote some of their time to coaching? Could job descriptions for assistant principals, curriculum coordinators, department chairs, deans, or others be modified to include coaching? Are there ways to adopt formal coaching positions, either by adding the positions if the budget allows or by repurposing existing positions?

A culture of coaching demands partnership, and there are cases in which such partnership is particularly challenging. Many coaches have asked us whether such a culture can thrive without a principal's active support. Many principals have asked us how to overcome powerful resistance among important leaders, including but not limited to the superintendent and other district leaders, school board members, teacher leaders, and teachers' unions. In these situations, educators can proceed only with caution and careful planning. Some may make the choice not to try. Others will believe that they have sufficient resources and support yet will fail and end up retreating, choosing to leave the school, or being asked to leave. Still others will try and succeed.

We have known schools in which passionate, capable coaches or teacher leaders have implemented coaching with little more than the tacit approval of the principal. We have also known principals who have withstood powerful resistance with resilience and dignity, weathering uncomfortable, even painful turbulence and making admirable progress. True transformation takes time. Even in the best cases, it is not a linear process. It requires maturity and the readiness to face numerous obstacles, especially in cultures that have long been characterized by professional isolation.

Keeping in mind that every situation and every school is different, in the following section we share three vignettes illustrating some of the challenges that principals may encounter in their quest to lead with a coach's hat.

## 1. When the Principal Is Not Open to Coaching

A first-year assistant principal who was primarily responsible for discipline in his school was surprised by the steady stream of students sent to his office by a single second-year math teacher. Deciding to investigate, he visited her classroom and quickly saw that although she had strong content knowledge and a warm demeanor, she lacked basic classroom management skills. After spending long hours on preparation and investing herself fully in students' success, she became frustrated when students responded to her informality with playful, disruptive banter. She would then show her agitation and habitually send students to the assistant principal. Based on informal conversations with this teacher, the assistant principal was confident that she was beginning to understand that sending students to him was undermining students' respect for her, and he anticipated that she would welcome support.

The assistant principal shared his thinking with the principal, explaining that he thought he could help this teacher by working with her much as an instructional coach would. He also shared some of his ideas for increasing collaboration among teachers: assigning master teachers as mentors for novices, creating opportunities for peer coaching, and setting up professional learning communities in which teachers could review data on students' academic and behavioral progress and work together to support student learning and growth. Teachers in the school were working in isolation, with no one entering their classrooms other than the principal, who came in once a year for a formal evaluation. They did not benefit from the observations of a supportive educator who could flag "blind spots," as instructional coaching expert Stephen Barkley calls them. In fact, they did not have anybody offering feedback on their classroom practice or helping them to improve.

The assistant principal was dismayed by his principal's reaction. The principal assured him that she would personally visit the teacher's classroom to observe the incompetence, write an unsatisfactory evaluation, and give the teacher a nonrenewal notice. She said that although she had not seen anything of sufficient concern the previous year to terminate the contract, she was certain she would now recognize the teacher's ineptitude and include it in her write-up. She also told the assistant principal that she did not want to burden him with the responsibility of coaching teachers on top of his disciplinary duties. She assured him that she was confident that in a short time, he would be able to handle all disciplinary problems promptly, keeping the school running smoothly and the teachers satisfied.

The assistant principal did not have the confidence to ask the principal all the questions he had: *What purpose does it serve to evaluate teachers if you are not going to provide them with support? Why give up so quickly on a teacher with potential? What effect does accepting responsibility for discipline have on teachers as professionals? When you spend time on routine classroom discipline in one particular classroom, how much of that time would be better spent on other areas that could promote school improvement?*

Several years passed, and the assistant principal grew increasingly frustrated. Eventually, he accepted a position at another school whose principal embraced his desire to incorporate coaching as a primary leadership approach. A few years later, he was hired to be a principal in another school. Among his first contributions was to create an instructional coaching program, hiring as his first instructional coaches some of the master teachers who had helped him during his first year as an administrator. Over the years, they created a powerful partnership and a culture of coaching that abounded with opportunities for active professional learning and collaboration among teachers.

## 2. When the Superintendent or School Board Is Not Open to Coaching

A principal who had worked as an instructional coach before being appointed to her current position reached out to a colleague in frustration. Committed to spending time in classrooms participating in learning and giving feedback to teachers, she had been instructed by her superintendent to focus on school management and formal evaluations. The superintendent made it clear that the principal's role was to keep the school safe and orderly and to ensure that teachers had the resources they needed and were held accountable for student learning, mostly as evidenced in test scores. He emphasized that the school board shared his perspective and that the principal's evaluation would be based on the quality of her skills as a manager and an evaluator.

Viewing herself primarily as an educator and a learning leader, the principal wondered whether she was in the right job. She considered resigning and seeking a position as an instructional coach or a teacher. In desperation, she shared her thoughts with a veteran principal colleague who encouraged her to stick it out at least for the year and see if she could find ways to infuse her current role with learning leadership. The colleague shared that she, too, was required to implement an evaluation system with two formal observations per year and substantial documentation, none of which she thought had any influence on teacher learning and effectiveness. She observed that feedback to teachers did not always need to be documented in the formal evaluation process. With the ongoing support of her colleague, the novice principal fulfilled the expectations of her superintendent and district while also offering teachers the opportunity for her to visit informally and meet to reflect on teaching and learning. A few teachers initially accepted her offer, and over time more and more teachers became interested. The principal tried unsuccessfully to secure funding to hire an instructional coach and to get permission to repurpose existing positions to offer some coaching to teachers. Nevertheless, she was able to meet district requirements for teacher evaluation while finding professional fulfillment through her support of teachers who appreciated the coaching she offered. She remained in her school for many years, gaining the respect of the teachers who worked closely with her.

### 3. When Teachers' Unions or Influential Teachers Are Not Open to Coaching

An experienced principal in her first year of a new position in a school with a strong teachers' union sought assistance from her own leadership coach. The district required one formal observation a year, and the union contract prohibited any informal observations beyond the one required for evaluation. "How can I nurture a culture of coaching," she asked her coach in exasperation, "when I am not even allowed to enter the classrooms?"

After some discussion with her coach, the principal met with the president of the teachers' union and said that she would like to invite a group of teachers to help plan job-embedded professional learning experiences. Recognizing that the meeting time for this professional development committee was beyond what was stipulated as required work in the teacher contract, the principal had already secured funding to pay teachers for their time. The union president consulted with the union board and, after some debate, they agreed that teachers could help the principal plan professional learning. Three teachers volunteered to participate in the planning process, but over the course of several months stopped attending meetings. They quietly let the principal know that they had been discouraged from participating by colleagues who felt that their participation made those who did not volunteer "look bad." The principal decided to build trust by entering classrooms, offering support, and showing appreciation. This worked out well: teachers expressed their gratitude for her support and recognition of the good work they were doing.

The following year, the principal continued her classroom observations, this time adding some questions for teacher reflection. She found that most teachers ignored her invitation to reflect, some politely thanked her, and one or two engaged in reflection, discussing ways to improve the quality of learning in their classrooms, brainstorming with the principal, and making changes to their practice based on their new insights. Later in the year, at a union meeting, several teachers complained that the informal observations violated the teacher contract and initiated a formal grievance. Although the district grievance committee determined that the principal's actions were contractually permitted, a number of teachers remained upset, and tension grew in the building.

The superintendent, who supported the principal's approach, transferred her to another school in the district whose faculty he believed would be open to exploring ways to improve their practice. The several teachers who had been working closely with the principal requested to be transferred with her, and the superintendent approved these requests. Together, along with some enthusiastic teachers in their new school, they made admirable progress engaging in peer coaching and professional learning communities to support student learning.

To replace the principal in the school she had left, the superintendent hired a kindhearted veteran principal who was reaching the end of his career and believed that the role of a school leader was to maintain order and keep teachers satisfied. The school staff members remained content with themselves and their practice and felt pleased to have a leader who kept them satisfied.

What all of these scenarios have in common is a lack of engagement and support from a key stakeholder. In each case, a talented educational leader faced a challenge, took it on with courage, and experienced the consequences: choosing to leave the school, being transferred to another school, or remaining and accepting the progress that was possible to achieve. Leading with a coach's hat is among the most powerful roles for a school leader, but it cannot be accomplished in cultures of isolation where principals and supervisors tend to their own responsibilities and teachers function with almost absolute autonomy, with limited opportunity for collaboration. Building a team within the building is essential for all leaders who want to foster the collaborative professional learning necessary to improve their schools' quality of learning and sense of community.

## Acknowledging the Vulnerability Inherent in Professional Learning

Acknowledging the vulnerability inherent in professional learning—indeed, in all learning—as educators open themselves to what they do not yet know and to whom they have not yet become is a daring and sometimes painful task. We understand educators' reluctance to open themselves up and reflect on their practice with a coach. Yet we aim to show teachers the celebratory exploration that beckons them, demanding a deep dive into their beliefs, perspectives, talents, and interests as well as their fears, insecurities, weaknesses, and limitations. Teaching, as we noted at the beginning of this chapter, is an act of courage. Likewise, coaching teachers is an act of bravery, as teachers are paradoxically sometimes the most reticent learners. Most school leaders who have been involved in professional learning have seen teachers' crossed arms, rolling eyes, glances at the clock, and distracted peeks at smartphones, which almost humorously mirror the disengaged behaviors of the teachers' own students.

There are many reasons for this impolite behavior, and the explanation may vary according to your perspective: from a sympathetic viewpoint, you might see teachers as jaded victims of decisions made by policymakers and administrators who are disconnected from the needs of students. From a more disdainful viewpoint, you could view teachers as uninspired and caring more about their own comfort than about students' needs. Neither of these perspectives, however, takes into account the unfolding learning process that leads toward growth or stagnation depending on the actions and interactions of all involved. True learning—not merely the performance required for a grade or a professional evaluation—requires the learner's full investment. Principal-coaches often choose to begin engaging teachers who have owned their own learning journey with courage and seek opportunities to expand their understanding and skills as a professional. Principal-coaches also determine ways to assist those who have not yet chosen to embark on a journey of professional exploration and who have no desire for a coach.

Touching on far more than pedagogy, effective principal-coaching helps teachers discover within themselves the qualities from which their professional talent stems. The process requires striving and depth, as poetically articulated by Parker Palmer in his 1998 book *The Courage to Teach*: "Good teaching," Palmer asserts, "cannot be reduced to technique; good teaching comes from the identity and integrity of the teacher" (p. 10). In his insightful reflection on what it means to coach and to be open to professional coaching, Palmer posits a series of questions that direct us toward a deeper understanding of the essence of teaching:

- The question we most commonly ask is the "what" question—what subjects shall we teach?
- When the conversation goes a bit deeper, we ask the "how" question—what methods and techniques are required to teach well?
- Occasionally, when it goes deeper still, we ask the "why" question—for what purpose and to what ends do we teach?
- But seldom, if ever, do we ask the "who" question—who is the self that teaches? How does the quality of my selfhood form—or deform—the way I relate to my students, my subject, my colleagues, my world? How can educational institutions sustain and deepen the selfhood from which teaching comes? (p. 4)

Principal-coaching at its most powerful guides teachers to reflect on the "who" questions, opening them to their own vulnerability and potential in ways both poignant and frightening. It is this duality—inherent in great coaching and great teaching—that transforms teacher support and evaluation into a far more complex and meaningful endeavor than is typically understood.

School cultures that are mature enough to embrace the process of empowering educators to stretch beyond their comfort zones will be the ones that ultimately model that same courageous process for students. Although we believe this transformation is possible for all schools, we also recognize that some schools can't overcome overwhelming challenges and obstacles, at least not yet. Journeys of professional learning and continuous school improvement are rarely, if ever, linear. Schools often encounter stalls, challenging turns, dead ends, or even complete stops. Some school cultures cling to the model of principal as evaluator and judge, whereas others cling to the model of principal as team captain. Still other schools view principals as managers, not particularly focused on teaching quality. As seen in the vignettes on pages 13–17, teachers and principals sometimes leave schools during the process, seeking cultures more receptive to their visions and ideals. Other times, teachers or principals are encouraged or even forced to leave as their efforts clash with their schools' culture and expectations. When transformational processes stall or fail even to begin, the result is typically a return to a comfortable status quo with which many educators, parents, and students are content. Yet when transformation does emerge, the results are inspirational. Students not only experience success but also embark on a process of lifelong self-discovery and self-expression, encouraged by the support and the example of their teachers.

Although we advise caution, stemming from our own implementation mistakes and failures as well as those of other talented educators with whom we have worked, we remain profoundly optimistic about the potential of principal-coaching to transform schools within a broader culture of coaching. Yes, schools will face challenges—poignantly human challenges. So many teachers have always functioned in isolation that it is downright unusual for teachers to work in the presence of colleagues or supervisors. Many schools do not embed regular time within the workday or even the work week for teachers to plan and reflect collaboratively. When other adults enter the classroom, teachers can feel misunderstood and threatened, and the visitors often feel like unwelcome intruders. One teacher we know told us that teachers in his school texted one another "POF" (principal on the floor) as a warning that the principal was conducting what they perceived as less-than-supportive classroom visits. Another of our trusted teacher colleagues shared that although she has an excellent working relationship with her principal, she still hates it when he conducts walkthroughs because she feels like she is onstage being observed and judged.

Just as teachers' vulnerability is too often ignored, so too is the vulnerability of principals. A MetLife survey of principals (Markow, Macia, & Lee, 2013) revealed that 75 percent of principals felt the job had become too complex; 69 percent said their job responsibilities were not very similar to what they had been five years previously; 48 percent felt great stress several days a week; and only 42 percent believed that they had a great deal of control over curriculum and instruction. The percentage of principals describing themselves as "very satisfied" with their jobs decreased nine points in five years, from 68 percent in 2008 to 59 percent in 2013.

Becoming open to vulnerability in the process of school improvement beckons principals to consider questions similar to those Parker Palmer posed about the essence of teaching:

• Who is the self that supervises, evaluates, coaches, mentors, inspires, articulates aspirations, sets expectations, and crafts robust supports?

• How does the quality of my selfhood form—or deform—the way I relate to my teachers, my aspirations for my school, my priorities, and my world?

• How can educational institutions sustain and deepen the selfhood from which learning leadership comes?

In a coaching relationship, the principal and teacher explore, learn, and grow together, revealing themselves to each other in the service of students. Principal-coaches strive to build relationships in which both teacher and principal appreciate and draw on each other's strengths while openly acknowledging their limitations and figuring out ways to expand their insight, understanding, and ability. Becoming a principal-coach requires far more reflection and focus on who you are as a professional than on the particular techniques you use. More significant than your "to-do" list is what is at the top of your "to-be" list. Read books on instructional coaching, and you will see certain qualities and attributes emerge repeatedly: effective instructional coaches build strong relationships, are good listeners, believe in teachers' potential, and are flexible, trustworthy, respectful, humble, responsive, self-reflective, and knowledgeable about best teaching practices. These characteristics do not differ essentially from those that define effective principals.

When you grapple with questions of personhood, you enhance teachers' sense of well-being as professionals while substantially improving the quality of learning, community, and culture in your school.

## The Benefits of Principal-Coaching

Coaching is nonnegotiable in the world of sports and increasingly commonplace in the world of business, yielding dramatic results: one Fortune 500 company assessed tangible and intangible benefits of leadership coaching for middle management and calculated a 529 percent return on investment (Anderson, 2001).

Yet school and district administrators as well as teachers are often skeptical of the benefits of coaching. Rick DuFour and Mike Mattos (2013) quote a study stating that three of four teachers report that their evaluation process has virtually no effect on their classroom practice. That is a chilling statistic. Principals spend a tremendous amount of time on evaluation, and that effort ought to have some influence on teacher effectiveness and student learning.

Within mandated evaluation processes, principals have room to include the opportunity for teacher reflection. DuFour and Mattos offer several options. One is to focus on team goals emphasizing student learning, thereby promoting the collaboration needed for individual teacher as well as school improvement. Another option is for the principal to use observations as opportunities to provide feedback to teachers on specific strategies that teachers have identified as goals for themselves—for example, checking for student understanding. Finally, DuFour and Mattos call on leaders to reframe their question from *How can I do a better job of monitoring teaching?* to *How can we collectively do a better job of monitoring student learning?*

The reframing of this question reflects a paradigm shift. Rather than hold dogmatic perspectives about how teaching should look, principal-coaching asks coaches and teachers to support students in whatever ways are needed to achieve their learning goals. In this position, educators strive to retain a curious and open stance toward the multiple pathways students may take to reach mastery.

John Hattie (2009) offers insights into how principals can most effectively bolster student learning in his investigation of more than 800 meta-analyses relating to student achievement, which represents the largest collection of evidence-based research into what actually works in schools. Citing a meta-analysis conducted by Robinson, Lloyd, and Rowe (2008) of 22 studies that include 2,833 principals, Hattie defines three distinct types of school leadership: transformational leadership, instructional leadership, and learning leadership:

- **Transformational leadership**, according to Hattie, is "inspiring teachers to new levels of energy and commitment towards a common mission, which develops the school's capacity to work together to overcome challenges and reach ambitious goals, and then to ensure that teachers have time to conduct their teaching" (p. 154). To us, this sounds great: inspiration, new levels of energy and commitment, a common mission, collaboration to reach ambitious goals, and respect for teaching time. Yet Hattie reports that the effect size of transformational leadership on student achievement is a mere 0.11, less than the effect size that would be expected with no intervention at all (0.40).

• **Instructional leadership**, according to Hattie, occurs among school leaders who "attend to the quality and impact of all in the school on student learning, ensure that disruption to learning is minimized, have high expectations of teachers for their students, visit classrooms, and are concerned with interpreting evidence about the quality and nature of learning in the school" (p. 154). To us, this also sounds quite good: a focus on student learning, high expectations, presence in classrooms, and attention to evidence about the quality of learning. Yet Hattie found that the effect size of instructional leadership was 0.42, barely above the 0.4 mark one could expect without any intervention.

• **Learning leadership**, according to Hattie, is leadership that emphasizes student and adult learning and occurs when leaders promote and participate in teacher learning by providing coaching over an extended period, forming data teams, focusing on how students learn subject-matter content, and enabling teachers to work collaboratively to plan and monitor lessons based on evidence about how students learn. In contrast with the minimal influence of transformational and instructional leadership, Hattie found the effect size of learning leadership to be an impressive 0.84, placing it as one of the most significant positive influences on student learning (see Figure 1.2).

The findings that support learning leadership's effectiveness in schools mirror the classroom findings. At the 2012 International Society for Technology in Education conference, educational researcher Michael Fullan, citing Hattie, relayed that *facilitative* teaching methods such as problem-based learning, simulations and gaming, and individualized instruction

Figure 1.2

## Effects of Different Types of School Leadership on Student Achievement

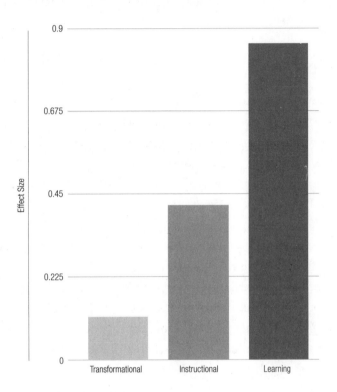

Based on data from Hattie (2012).

have only a 0.17 effect size on student learning—less than anticipated with no intervention at all. In contrast, *activating* learning by offering feedback, accessing thinking, supporting students in setting and reaching challenging goals, and monitoring learning has a 0.84 effect size on student learning—one of the most effective interventions Hattie found.

Going beyond the well-worn educational goal of moving from "sage on the stage" to "guide on the side," Hattie compels leaders to view themselves as activators rather than mere facilitators of learning. We have come to call this expanded role a "coach to approach." Unlike facilitating learning, activating learning requires the teacher or coach to support deliberate change and growth and to demonstrate the effect of learning experiences on student and teacher outcomes.

## Conclusion

If a school were a sports team, what would the principal be?

Judge? Captain? Manager? Owner? Sportscaster?

Physical therapist? Cheerleader? Groundskeeper? Promoter? Fan?

We believe principals can be more than managers and judges, more than professionals responsible for maintaining discipline and evaluating teachers. Principals can become lead learners, supporting teachers to be more effective both as individual professionals within their classrooms and as members of a team of educators functioning collaboratively for the benefit of all students. This shift requires principals to learn new techniques, many adopted from the approaches of instructional coaching. Even more important than techniques, however, are the leaders' active ownership of professional priorities and a strong focus on the actions that will most likely enhance their schools' quality of learning and community.

Leading with a coach's hat is a redefinition of the role of leader. Wearing the coach's hat, leaders adopt approaches that will enable their schools to be more effective and agile as they address a wide range of student needs in the present while preparing students for success in the rapidly changing world they will inherit. We welcome you to embark on the process of change for the sake of your teachers and your students.

# Put On Your Coach's Hat

*Reflect on your practice:*

- What is your current leadership type? Transformational, instructional, learning, or some combination of these?
- How closely do your current practices align with leading with a coach's hat?
- What practices do you want to change to get closer to leading with a coach's hat?
- What concerns or hesitations do you have about leading with a coach's hat? What potential challenges do you see in your future as you put on your coach's hat?
- What type of feedback have you received in your evaluations as a teacher or an administrator? Was that feedback helpful?
- Whom do you need to talk to about what you would like to change? For example, the superintendent, staff members, the assistant principal?

*Next steps:*

- Find trusted colleagues with whom you can reflect on what the role of principal can be.
- Write two job descriptions for yourself: one based on what you currently do and the other describing what you would like your job description as a learning leader and principal-coach to be.
- Write a list of questions and reflections about what you would like to know about coaching. As you read the rest of this book, jot down answers for yourself.

---------- TWO ----------

# Putting On Your Coach's Hat

When you watch a practice session for any sport, you can easily identify a good coach. She or he is constantly giving feedback to the team as a whole as well as to individual players, engaging in conversations, and building players' skills and confidence. The coach observes as players take on new skills or hone existing ones and offers feedback that is both positive and focused on growth.

As we dig into what it means to put on your coach's hat, let's look at the story of Chris, a first-year principal eager to start his new role as a learning leader.

### A Principal's Perspective

Many teachers decide to move into school leadership after being inspired by a great leader. Chris was different: he aspired to be a principal *despite* his own principal's lack of learning leadership. After years of working in a building with colleagues just as frustrated as he was, Chris assumed his new role of principal with the goal of doing the opposite of what his former principal had done.

Chris began by scheduling individual meetings with teachers to help him build relationships and learn about their passions and the school's strengths and challenges. Determined to be prepared to support his staff, he also researched the literacy program his school had just adopted. During a back-to-school professional development training on the program, Chris participated right along with the teachers. It was important for him to know what to look for during classroom observations and to be able to reflect with teachers on successes and obstacles. During trainings in his former school, the principal had routinely sat in the back corner of the room checking his e-mail, completely unaware of what the teachers were being trained on; not surprisingly, the school had been notorious for its failure to follow through on initiatives. In Chris's new school, he began his practice of visiting classrooms from day one to give teachers recognition for the strengths he saw in their teaching and to offer feedback on their implementation of the new literacy program.

As the school year progressed, Chris was able to tailor professional development trainings to more effectively meet faculty's needs because he was so attuned to the overall level of implementation across the school. It was not unusual for him to offer to co-teach a lesson with a teacher or to cover a classroom so that a teacher could observe a colleague's class.

Teachers at Chris's new school began noticing the difference that his commitment to learning alongside them made, and many expressed appreciation of his active presence. Others were more skeptical of these practices. Through it all, Chris remained positive and stayed the course. His main goal during his first year was to listen, build relationships, and learn with and among teachers and students. He continually looked for ways to immerse himself in the work of the school.

Although Chris had had no prior experience with coaching, he clearly led with a coach's hat. When we walk through schools, we can easily identify principals or other supervisors who have this leadership style: they're the ones who are entering classrooms, speaking with students about their learning, writing reflective notes to teachers, discussing teaching and learning with teachers both individually and in groups, and participating in collaborative learning experiences with teachers.

In this chapter, we explore how to get started as a principal-coach. Because the crucial first step is to get out of your office, we focus on strategies to help you conduct frequent, informal classroom visits, offer feedback to teachers, and overcome common obstacles to these goals. We invite you to put on your coach's hat and get in the game.

## Step 1: Get Out of Your Office

Getting out of the office can be challenging. The office's gravitational pull seems to compel principals to spend their days attending meetings, returning e-mails and phone calls, and completing paperwork. Principals are expected to serve as educational visionaries, curriculum designers, data analysts, disciplinarians, relationship builders, faculty and staff supervisors, resource allocators, facilities managers, schedulers, special event planners, public relations and communications directors, community builders, and conflict and crisis resolvers. Much of this work happens in their offices.

To complicate matters, principals are evaluated both formally and informally by many different stakeholders—superintendents, school boards, parents, teachers, and students—whose priorities often vary. Many members of our schools and communities hold deeply ingrained, often unexamined perceptions about what principals should do. Principals often feel frustrated by the discrepancy between the level of accountability they're held to and the level of influence they actually have on many factors affecting school success. Adding to the difficulties, principals struggle with a sense of isolation, workloads that seem insurmountable, and inadequate supports (National Association of Secondary School Principals & National Association of Elementary School Principals, 2013).

Too often, principals are so overwhelmed with work that they are grateful when they can put in a full day in the office, productively engaged and checking items off their to-do lists. Yet when they pause and take the time to wonder about their effect as leaders, they often realize that they need to reconsider their priorities: visiting classrooms and getting involved in teaching and learning has a far greater influence than almost any other responsibility.

## Preparing for Classroom Visits and Clarifying Purpose

The first concrete task of a principal-coach is to get out of the office and walk into classrooms. Just as a teacher spends the first few weeks of school getting to know her or his students and building classroom community, a principal taking on this new paradigm of leadership must begin developing a "classroom visitation rapport" with teachers and students. Visiting classrooms will help you to get to know each student, become acquainted with each teacher's strengths and instructional style, learn the curriculum for each grade level, and put your finger on the pulse of what is happening in the building. If you know your teachers only from interactions in meetings or your annual or even triennial formal observations, getting into their classrooms will lead you to see them in a new light. If you know students only from saying "hello" and "good-bye" at arrival and dismissal and from disciplinary interactions, you will likely begin to see them in a different light as well.

Both classroom visits and ensuing feedback and conversation should be informal and nonjudgmental, not documented for the formal evaluation system. This, we recognize, can be a challenging concept for many administrators to accept, especially in systems that promote a "document, document, document!" mentality. Keep in mind that these visits are intended to keep you informed of what is occurring in the classroom, to help you get to know students and teachers, and to enable you to guide teachers to reflect on their practice.

Before making classroom visits a regular habit, you will need to inform teachers of your purpose for being in their classrooms. If you just enter a classroom without explanation, you will likely disrupt that class. Either the teacher will stop the lesson to greet you and ask what you need, or a student will announce to the teacher that you're there.

You owe it to your staff to address the changes you're making, and how you do it will make all the difference. If you simply *tell* your staff about your intention to come into their classrooms on a regular basis, you are bound to encounter resistance. Staff may become uneasy about your visits and even question your intentions. If you decide to *show* your staff your intentions just by appearing in their classrooms on a regular basis, the same uneasy feelings may prevail. Chances are you would feel the same if your supervisor started showing up in your school without warning or explanation.

We recommend a third path: engaging with faculty, sharing your intentions to be in classrooms, following through by making classroom engagement a priority, and seeking feedback both directly and indirectly on your classroom visits and participation. When you meet with teachers, explain that just as an athletic coach is invested in the success of individual players and the team as a whole, you are invested in the success of each teacher as well as the entire school. Make it clear that your goal is not to evaluate but to reflect on the teaching and learning happening in their classrooms and to offer feedback to facilitate their professional learning. Tell teachers that they should assume that when you offer observations and feedback, you are speaking to them as a coach. Let them know that if you ever have a concern as an evaluator, you will let the teacher know that you are wearing your "evaluator's hat" rather than your "coach's hat." Here is how one principal we know explains classroom visits to her teachers:

An instructional coach's role is to improve instruction, and I don't see my role any differently; I just also happen to have many other duties to fulfill as well. I recognize that when I come in your classroom and send you an e-mail or talk to you afterward, it may make you feel nervous or worried—which is *not* my intent! When I come into classrooms for informal class visits, I am coming in with a "coach's hat" on, so to speak. I may pose a question to you that stretches your thinking and that is not meant to be intrusive or evaluative, but to have you reflect on why you do what you do. When you are reflective and aware of why you do what you do, you will continue to utilize effective strategies for students in your classroom. So, my key message to you is that unless I specifically say, "I have a concern," then you have nothing to be concerned about. I am just in there wearing my "coach's hat."

One way to overcome teachers' reluctance to invite administrators into their classrooms is to collaboratively identify "look-fors" that should be present in the class, thus ensuring that everyone is on the same page and has some agency in the process. In one particular school that Kathy worked in, the principal and instructional coach worked with the entire staff to develop common look-fors that should be occurring during a literacy block. The teachers and principal worked collaboratively to answer the following questions:

1. Based on what we know about quality instruction and the components of literacy instruction, what should be observable in a classroom during the literacy block?

2. If someone visited a classroom at various times during the block, what type of data would be helpful for you, the teacher, to receive?

3. How could these visits help teachers reflect on their practices and grow to new levels?

The building leadership team then took the ideas and generated a data collection tool (see Figure 2.1, p. 34).

Figure 2.1

## Literacy Look-Fors

Observer: _____

| Teacher: _____ | | Date: _____ | | Grade: _____ | | Time: _____ | |
|---|---|---|---|---|---|---|---|

| Component: | ___ PA | ___ Phonics | ___ Comp | ___ Fluency | ___ Vocab | ___ Writing | ___ Other* |
|---|---|---|---|---|---|---|---|
| Grouping: | ___ Whole | ___ Small | ___ Pairs | ___ Individual | *Specify the other: | | |

| | | |
|---|---|---|
| **Explicit Instruction:** | ___ Yes (*Check Component Observed:*)<br>___ Introduction; ___ Modeling; ___ Guided Practice; ___ Application | ___ Not at this time |
| **Eyes on Print:** | ___ # of students are currently reading text/ ___ total # of students in class | ___ Not at this time |
| **Teacher Talk:** | ___ Teacher-directed talk/telling      ___ Coaching; student interaction; scaffolding | **Materials being used:** |
| **Engagement:** | ___ # of students are engaged in meaningful tasks/ ___ total # of students in class | |
| **Comments:** | | |

Instead of having the principal just start using the tool, the instructional coach provided opportunities for staff members to try it out while observing one another and then to engage in follow-up conversations. Teachers became comfortable with having visitors in their classrooms, and the process of observing and being observed showed them that these types of classroom visits were not meant to be evaluative. They realized that they could learn from the data collected and, more important, from the dialogue that followed.

## Planning and Prioritizing

When you first step out of your office and into teachers' classrooms, you will need to get into the habit of scheduling classroom time, figuring out what to do during classroom visits—which range from approximately 5 minutes to 45 minutes long—and getting to know each of your teachers as professionals in their own classrooms. Developing these habits is much like starting a new exercise program: it may feel unnatural at first, and it takes planning and effort, but if you stick with it, the process will become smoother and you will get better. The famous Nike slogan "Just do it!" applies here: despite your misgivings or compelling reasons for not being able to leave the office, it's so important to just get into the classroom. The benefits far outweigh the challenges.

That said, successfully sustaining the practice of visiting classrooms does require some planning and discipline. Make sure you schedule time deliberately to be present in classrooms and not let that time be swallowed up by meetings, paperwork, or even crises. We recognize that some demands and, yes, crises are unavoidable, but try to respect classroom time as much as you do other commitments. If you would not cancel a meeting with a parent or teacher to deal with an unforeseen demand or crisis, don't cancel classroom time, either. Some principals find it valuable to schedule time every day for classroom visits, at different times of the day. Others schedule time throughout the week. Determine a schedule that makes sense given the rhythm of your own work week, and experiment with it to see what is most effective for you. (We dig deeply into time management in Chapter 5.)

## Classroom Visits: How to Conduct Them and Follow Up

Once you're in the classroom, make an effort to recognize and appreciate the strengths in each educator's teaching style. Build teachers' comfort level with your presence by offering compliments in a one-on-one follow-up conversation or in a note. Don't worry yet about areas that may need improvement (unless, of course, you witness unacceptable or harmful behaviors). Be prepared to laugh. On one of Shira's early classroom visits, she entered a 3rd grade classroom to find the teacher scrounging through the garbage can while some students huddled around her and others socialized with one another. When the teacher looked up at Shira, her face turned red with embarrassment. "I'm looking for a tooth," she nervously explained. One of the students had lost a tooth and accidentally thrown it away and was anxious to find it so that she could bring it home to her mother. Shira reassured the teacher and told her not to worry, and afterward the two had a good laugh about the "lesson." Shira also made sure to return to the class the next day and complimented the teacher on her approaches that did not include digging in the garbage. She also complimented the teacher on the care with which she had treated a distressed child. There can be strength in the unexpected.

When in classrooms, strive to be fully present. If you are concerned about the feedback you are giving teachers after classroom visits, fear not: we address this in Chapter 4. Before you can focus on quality feedback, you have to develop the routine of being in classrooms. The more often you are in classrooms, the easier it gets to quietly enter without the students or teacher even noticing you. If your entry into a classroom ever seems to disrupt the flow of the lesson, with the teacher greeting you or students asking what you're doing, it may indicate that you haven't been visiting that classroom enough.

## Being Open to Teachers' Perspectives

The following vignette illustrates, from a teacher's point of view, how a skilled principal-coach initiated classroom visits that prompted the teacher to reflect deeply on her practice.

### A Teacher's Perspective

Kristen had taught at Washington Elementary for seven years and felt confident in her expertise as a teacher. From conversations with her colleagues, she concluded that she knew the curriculum better than anyone, and she often helped her fellow teachers with their planning. She worked hard every day to plan, teach, grade papers, maintain contact with parents, and lead several different event committees for the entire school. The school's previous principal was not a learning leader and had visited Kristen's classroom only a couple of times but had recognized Kristen's hard work in a glowing evaluation that highlighted her commitment to committees and the time she spent working before and after school.

Within the first few months of Mrs. Jones's tenure as principal of Washington Elementary, the teachers were discussing with one another how many times she had already been in their classrooms. Some teachers appreciated that Mrs. Jones had sent them notes complimenting their teaching, but others had questions about what was happening in their classrooms. They couldn't help but wonder exactly what Mrs. Jones's agenda was.

The first few times Kristen noticed Mrs. Jones in her classroom, she felt intimidated by the prospect of having someone watching and possibly scrutinizing her, even though Mrs. Jones would follow up by leaving her positive notes that made her day. Whereas Kristen's previous principal had recognized how much time she spent at work, Mrs. Jones recognized her effective classroom management and use of cooperative grouping.

After the third visit, Mrs. Jones asked to meet with Kristen. During their conversation, Mrs. Jones shared her observations about the questions Kristen had asked during her lesson and noted that Kristen had called on only a couple of students. "How dare she come in and criticize my teaching?" was Kristen's immediate thought. But then Mrs. Jones asked questions that prompted Kristen to reflect: how could she know which students understood the content and which ones didn't when she called on only the highest-achieving students? Had she ever noticed that calling on a student to answer a question let the rest of the class off the hook for even thinking about the question? They talked through some new questioning strategies for Kristen to try in her classroom. As she implemented the new strategies, Kristen was amazed by the difference they made in her students' learning and was excited to see Mrs. Jones pop in to her classroom to see her using the strategies. During their follow-up discussion, Mrs. Jones complimented Kristen on her use of the techniques and then began to discuss the two English language learners in her classroom, who seemed to be struggling. Mrs. Jones helped Kristen identify a couple of strategies that would help these two students be more successful while also benefiting the class as a whole.

Although some of the critical comments in the faculty lounge continued, Kristen recognized that the negativity stemmed from teachers' insecurity, which she had also felt at first. Unlike Kristen, these teachers hadn't yet realized that they were finally receiving feedback that would help them improve their teaching and students' learning. Their previous principal had come into their classrooms only to write up formal evaluations that just kept them doing what they had always done. Kristen now looked forward to Mrs. Jones's visits because she knew that the observations would help her see things she hadn't noticed before and come up with strategies to improve student learning in her classroom.

Responses to an anonymous online survey we conducted asking teachers about nonevaluative feedback from their principals support our belief in the value of leading with a coach's hat. Comments included the following:

• "I would love more conversation between principals and teachers. If the discussion is informal and constructive, who knows how much more growth we would see in the teachers and the principals? I love when my principal just stops by. I even ask for this, but it rarely happens!"

• "I had one evaluation in my first seven years of teaching. And the feedback came four weeks after observation!"

• "Right now, my principal only comes in my room for evaluations (be they formal or informal). How I interpret that is that she does not care about my growth as a teacher, but just needs to evaluate me for the powers that be. I think that if my principal came and provided me with feedback in a nonevaluative way, I could grow and benefit as an educator."

• "I think that the more feedback teachers receive, the better they will be as practitioners. It is critical that teachers know that their principals know and care for them and have a clear understanding of what is going well or not so well in the classroom. Nonevaluative feedback is a key component that makes evaluative feedback unsurprising."

- "I love the idea of classroom walkthroughs; it puts less pressure on evaluations when a principal has seen more than one or two lessons in the span of a year!"

- "I think the principal needs to be highly visible to the students throughout the day, and having regular visits shows the students how important classroom time is. It also holds the teacher accountable for high-quality teaching all the time. We've all worked across the hall from the 'cool' teacher who has free days when the principal is out!"

As noted previously, some teachers are not yet aware of the benefits of effective classroom visits; others may feel suspicious or nervous about them. Tentative or even dismissive reactions to coaching tend to occur when schools have not yet created a serious culture of professional learning. Such a culture takes time to develop. While remaining enthusiastic about the value of leading with a coach's hat, make sure that you're attentive to the concerns of those you serve as well as to their sometimes-different conceptions of what a principal's role should be.

### The Importance of Support for Principals

Prominent literacy expert Regie Routman writes in *Read, Write, Lead* (2014) about her residencies in schools where she would spend each day modeling instruction to help teachers improve their literacy practices. She described one school in particular where she had completed a weeklong residency with teachers twice each year over a four-year period. Although the school had made achievement gains both on state and district tests and in daily writing, some teachers continued to resist the literacy practices she had modeled, not even teaching writing every day. Routman realized that although the principal was a strong leader, she rarely left her office to observe classes and offer feedback. It was this realization that led Routman to change the format of her weeklong residencies: instead of working with teachers the entire day, she would spend the morning working with teachers and the afternoon mentoring the principal. She has found that this change has made a big difference in short- and long-term outcomes in the schools she works with.

The support that Routman provided to principals is sadly unusual. Although teachers often work in isolation, they do communicate with and rely on one another. In many schools, faculty rooms serve as centers in which teachers find companionship, even if it's not always healthy or supportive. The principal, upon whom a multitude of concerns, fears, hopes, expectations, and aspirations rests, has no such support. As principals nurture a culture of reflection and learning and advocate coaching for all professionals, they must also secure support for themselves. Such supports can include engaging and collaborating with district leadership and teachers to identify challenges and possible solutions as well as finding a coach of their own, whether a professional leadership coach, a peer, or a combination, to support their reflection and learning. Some districts and schools allocate professional development funding for principals to receive coaching. Alternatively, principals can organize peer coaching models for themselves with colleagues they trust and respect.

## Overcoming Obstacles

Principals often find that making the switch to the coach's hat is an overwhelming experience. In the beginning, they may fear that they've just increased their workload from "too heavy" to "insurmountable." With time and practice, leading with a coach's hat will actually make your job easier, but in this section, we address the two most common objections we hear: "I don't have time to do more observations than the minimum!" and

"How can I visit classrooms when I'm always dealing with student discipline issues?"

## Obstacle 1: I don't have time to do more observations than the minimum!

Every teacher evaluation system is different. However, with the constantly changing political climate and its attendant shifts in educational priorities (see, for example, Response to Intervention, Race to the Top, No Child Left Behind waivers, the Common Core, and the Every Student Succeeds Act) and testing requirements, many states have moved toward a uniform system of teacher evaluation. Such systems require principals to conduct a certain number of formal and informal observations of teachers based on teaching standards, using specific forms and additional documentation. Teacher evaluation systems tend not to ask principals to make regular classroom visits to provide formative feedback and hold informal conversations focused on improving learning. Instead, they generally set up a framework of minimum requirements.

We encourage principals to treat these minimum requirements as just that: the bare minimum that they must do for their teachers. The new evaluation system in Jessica's district requires her to conduct two formal and five informal observations of each teacher over the course of three years to complete a summative evaluation during the third year of the evaluation cycle. When Jessica went through training for this new system, she was astounded to hear an administrative team from another district trying to decide if it could "outsource" the formal observations to external evaluators because the principals were so busy already. If principals using this system fulfilled the minimum requirements for observations, they would be in each teacher's classroom just twice a year; over the course of three years, the time required would add up to less than 1 percent of each classroom's teaching and learning time. Yes, principals are busy—but when did they get so busy that observing just 1 percent of classroom time is too much?

Fulfilling these minimum requirements will not help teachers to improve teaching and learning in their classrooms; it will simply help you meet your own paperwork requirements. Whatever your teacher evaluation system is, we encourage you to get into classrooms as much as possible to provide teachers with informal feedback and opportunities to reflect on their practice and student outcomes. If you're shaking your head right now and thinking, *I don't have* time *to do more than I'm required to do,* hear us out: in the long run, doing more than the minimum will actually lighten your load and make you a more effective, efficient evaluator.

The problem with sticking to the minimum number of required observations is that you may not get an accurate snapshot of the teacher's practice. If your classroom visits are rare, you might be fooled by a mediocre teacher's "dog and pony show" and miss a valuable opportunity to provide feedback that would help him or her to grow. Conversely, you might catch a great teacher on a bad day and erroneously assume the worst.

When you visit classrooms frequently, you will see the good, the bad, and the ugly—and you will know when you need to give feedback, when you need to give support, and when you need to document your observations for dismissal. You will know immediately when an ineffective teacher is putting on a performance, and you will know when an effective teacher is having an off day that you don't need to document. Good teachers will appreciate your familiarity with their practice and be more willing to take risks in the classroom. When it comes time to schedule formal observations, your best teachers will tell you, "Come in whenever."

We do recognize that finding time for these visits isn't easy amid all the other demands on your time—not least of which are the additional components of learning leadership, including planning with teachers and providing support to other school leaders. This is why it is vital to set up a schedule that allocates time not only to visit classrooms but also to offer feedback and engage in short reflective conversations with teachers.

We also recognize that even principals who wear the coach's hat aren't actually coaches. An instructional coach is able to spend extended amounts of time with individual teachers during coaching cycles and have a tremendous influence on teachers' professional growth. By contrast, the ongoing feedback that a principal can provide throughout the school year will come in small, informal doses after short, unannounced classroom visits. We, along with other principals we know, have set a goal of getting into classrooms two hours a day; however, during major testing seasons, busy programmatic times, or unanticipated crises, we do not always meet our goal. But we do not then throw the goal out the window like a New Year's resolution to exercise more. Instead, we try again the next day.

## Obstacle 2: How can I visit classrooms when I'm always dealing with student discipline issues?

One of the most common reasons principals give for not being able to visit classrooms each day is that they're constantly attending to student discipline issues. Whether you are the lone administrator in your building or you have an assistant principal or a dean of students, student discipline issues (along with other "fires" to put out) are a reality in any school.

We have found from our own experience that the more time the principal spends visiting classrooms, the fewer discipline incidents there are to spend time on. However, we realize that this can present a catch-22 in the short term: how can you find the time to visit classrooms to help teachers with classroom management when the teachers are continuously sending students to your office?

When a teacher sends a student to the office, it is because the situation has gotten beyond his or her control. When a teacher *repeatedly* sends a student to your office, it is because he or she does not know what to do with that student or because what he or she is doing is not working. In any of these cases, teachers need your guidance on how to move forward and possibly some additional strategies to add to their toolbox. Your goal should always be to get the student back into the classroom and help the teacher know how to move forward with this student in the classroom.

When teachers constantly send students to the office, it's safe to assume that they are the problem, not the students—but it will not be helpful to just tell teachers to get their classrooms under control. If they knew how to, they would have done so already! In these situations, it is best to help the teacher come up with some short-term steps based on the specific student needs *and* to tell the teacher that you plan to get into his or her classroom more frequently to observe the "problem" student, especially during the times when the student typically gets into trouble. While you are in the classroom to observe the student, make sure that you are observing the teacher even more. Be on the lookout for what precedes the student's misbehavior as well as the teacher's response to the student. Unless the student has a significant emotional disability that affects his or her behavior, it is likely that you will be able to identify practices that the teacher can change to help improve the student's behavior. You may also find that the teacher's instructional method is generally unengaging and that the student is misbehaving out of boredom or lack of purpose. In such cases, you may find yourself surprised that there are not *more* student issues.

No teacher *wants* to have poor classroom management skills. When you see a teacher struggling with classroom management, why not offer the feedback and support that they need to improve? By helping teachers to improve their classroom management, you are helping them to maximize learning in their classroom, now and for all their future students.

While continuing to give feedback to teachers who struggle with classroom management, make sure to visit classrooms where there are students who have a history of behavior issues. We often refer to these students as our "frequent flyers." Make a point to connect with these students in a positive way before they end up in your office for the wrong reason. Put each student's name on your calendar or morning to-do list until you've developed the habit of checking in with each student at the start of the day.

Even if you are currently dealing with a deluge of student discipline issues in your building, the time has come to stop using that as an excuse to stay in your office and instead to use it as a reason to get into the classrooms that students are being sent out of. Give teachers the feedback and support they need so that you can spend the time *you* need to in all of your classrooms.

## Planting Seeds to Inspire Growth

Planting seeds in a garden and watching them transform can be an invigorating process. Each new stage is something to celebrate and enjoy. Over time, with proper nurturing, small seeds can grow into a beautiful garden.

Educators are constantly planting seeds in their professional lives. Principals who lead with a coach's hat have opportunities to transform the educational landscape.

Once you have spent ample time observing in classrooms, you can help teachers reflect and expand on their practices through short "seed-planting" sessions. We met Chris at the beginning of this chapter. Let's take a look at how he planted a seed.

Chris enjoyed spending time in classrooms and making note of approaches he saw teachers using over time. As he visited Sue's 4th grade classroom throughout the year, he became impressed with her use of student notebooks during writing workshop. These notebooks served as a place for students to gather their thoughts and share during their "author's chair" moments. He noticed that the practice was helping students gain confidence in their writing and wondered if there was a way their writing could reach a larger audience. He had recently started a blog for himself and noticed that another teacher on staff had his students blogging regularly. Chris wondered if Sue had considered providing students with such a platform for their writing.

Chris soon found an opportunity to talk informally with Sue when she dropped by his office. He noted that he enjoyed observing her use of student notebooks and listening to students sharing their writing. Because he had visited Sue's classroom regularly, he was able to provide a few examples of students' growth. He then asked if she had noticed any students gaining confidence in their writing from sharing their writing with others. Sue shared a brief story about her shy student Cory, who lit up when classmates complimented his writing. She noted that students were starting to offer one another revision suggestions, and this student-to-student interaction was helping Cory become more confident in other areas as well.

Chris didn't want to extend the visit too long, but he mentioned that Steve, a 5th grade teacher, had recently started having his students share their writing through a blog. The students' writing was beginning to gain an audience not only of their parents but also of students and teachers in other parts of the country and even throughout the world.

The seed Chris planted took root. Sue was eager to visit with Steve to learn more about student blogging. In no time, she had incorporated student blogs into her writer's workshop, and her new love of blogging led to other forms of technology integration. One seed not only flourished in Sue's classroom but also transformed the school's educational landscape as other teachers began contacting Steve and Sue for advice on setting up student blogs!

Some teachers, like Sue, take a suggestion and run with it. Other times, the seeds you plant will need more nurturing. Still other seeds may need to be dropped and new seeds sown in other areas. Your job as principal-coach is not to be the one with all the answers; your job is to watch for strengths, listen, ask questions, look for possibilities, and inspire teachers to grow. In Chapter 4, we discuss the role of growth conversations with teachers in further depth.

## Conclusion

Although this book is about principals acting more as instructional coaches than as supervisors, we do want to reiterate that it is impossible for the principal to be seen purely as an instructional coach would. At the end of the day—or at the end of whatever deadline is given by the school district—the principal is still the evaluator who has the power to issue a notice of nonrenewal or dismissal. The principal is still the person in the building who must address issues like frequent teacher tardiness or unprofessional conduct. Still, even if you have teachers who are past the point of help, your ultimate goal should be to serve as instructional coach and learning leader for the rest of your staff.

Explain to teachers that you will be wearing your "coach's hat" unless you explicitly state that you are discussing a concern as a supervisor. With teachers who are advancing in their careers, making contributions, and continuing to improve their practice, you can focus on coaching, even when you conduct district-mandated formal evaluations. When teachers *are* in the process of potential nonrenewal, they should know that you are acting as an evaluator and have access to the support of others—including, if possible, an instructional coach—who do not have evaluative responsibility.

Whether they say it outright or not, teachers need feedback to help them grow as professionals and improve the learning in their classrooms. As you, teachers, and students become accustomed to your new active role in the classroom, you will find that you have your finger on the pulse of everything happening in the building. You will now be ready to put on your coach's hat and provide teachers with informal feedback on their professional growth goals or their implementation of a new school initiative and engage in reflective dialogue focused on improving student learning.

Whatever the requirements of your evaluation system are, we challenge you to do more than the minimum. We challenge you to focus more on the opportunity to engage in coaching dialogue than on getting bogged down in the paperwork (although it is important to complete what's required!). We challenge you to be a regular presence in classrooms and to wear your coach's hat more often than you wear your evaluator's hat.

To sum up, we encourage you to

• Inform teachers of your purpose for making classroom observations, and then get out of your office and into classrooms to build a "classroom visitation rapport."

• Visit classrooms as much as possible, going beyond the minimum number of observations required by your evaluation system.

• Schedule time in your daily or weekly calendar to be in classrooms, and treat those visits as a priority, just as you would any other important meeting.

• Visit the classrooms of teachers struggling with student discipline issues and provide feedback and strategies to help ensure that students stay in their classrooms for learning.

## Put On Your Coach's Hat

*If getting into classrooms is a new practice for you:*

• Talk to your staff about your new goal of making classroom visits and providing informal feedback. Announce it at the next staff meeting, or e-mail it out now. Make sure to let your staff know that your intent is to observe and support, not to evaluate.

• Schedule your classroom time for the next two weeks. Vary the time each day so that you aren't always visiting a classroom at the same time.

• Start by visiting the classrooms of your new teachers and your most positive teachers. They will help spread the word that your visits aren't so scary.

*If getting into classrooms is a regular practice for you:*

• If you haven't already done so, share your intentions with your teachers and explain the coach's hat concept to them.

- Try different methods of giving feedback: have a conversation with one teacher, leave a handwritten note in another teacher's mailbox, and e-mail feedback to another. Which method do you prefer? Which method do you think teachers prefer? Which method do you think is most feasible for you to use frequently?

- Try following up a few observations with short reflective conversations. Look for opportunities to plant seeds. Make note of transformations, and keep encouraging teachers to build on strengths.

# Three

# Building Successful Coaching Relationships

*Great schools grow when educators understand that the power of*
*their leadership lies in the strength of their relationships.*

—Gordon Donaldson (2007)

Relationships are the heart of a school—and those between a principal-coach and his or her teachers are among the most dynamic and nuanced as well as potentially the most rewarding. Looking back, we can think of many insights that we wish we'd had when we embarked on our own principal-coaching journeys. More than anything, though, we wish that we had been more honest with ourselves in acknowledging the complexity and importance of our relationships with teachers.

Any leader who has tried to implement an improvement effort or a new initiative can attest to the role school culture plays in the initiative's success or failure. Even positive school cultures are delicate and require careful tending. Navigating an evolving school culture can be especially challenging; it's not something that can be mapped out and strategized. As the saying commonly attributed to management guru Peter Drucker goes, "Culture eats strategy for breakfast."

School culture is a complex amalgam of countless influences (e.g., teachers, students, the district office) and factors (e.g., state and federal policies, budgets and shifting economics, community events and societal changes, challenges and successes in the lives of students and their families) that cannot be controlled by building leaders. That said, principals *do* have considerable influence in developing positive, productive relationships with teachers. Finding ways to nurture these relationships is central to successfully leading with a coach's hat.

In our own efforts to build positive relationships and school culture, we have been inspired by numerous thinkers' exploration of trust. In *The Speed of Trust* (2006), Stephen M. R. Covey describes trust as a pragmatic, tangible, actionable asset that can be created rather quickly. David Horsager, author of *The Trust Edge* (2011), concurs, describing trust as a measurable competency that incorporates reliability, dependability, and capability. Megan Tschannen-Moran, author of *Trust Matters* (2004), defines trust as "one's willingness to be vulnerable to another based on the confidence that the other is benevolent, honest, open, reliable, and competent" (p. 17).

We devoured these and other works on trust and implemented their guidance with as much fidelity as we could muster. We did see benefits, certainly. Yet in some ways, these perspectives on trust paradoxically led us astray, causing us to believe that if we were consistent and skilled, respectful and kind, patient and understanding, we would earn the trust of our teachers. Ultimately, we found these attributes essential but insufficient.

Coaching conversations push us to go beyond these qualities and make ourselves vulnerable. On the surface, these conversations grapple with curriculum and pedagogic techniques, but at a deeper level, they are expressions of our core beliefs about teaching, learning, students, and ourselves. When we were able to discuss our differing perspectives openly, with respectful curiosity, creative solutions were born. However, when our distinct views, so central to our personal vision and identity, remained implicit and unexplored—even when we embodied all the important qualities listed above—what tended to emerge were painful misunderstandings and mistrust.

To be completely transparent, we found this chapter difficult to write. There is no one-size-fits-all recipe to building coaching relationships in the school setting. Every school brings a unique set of ingredients to the table, and no two are exactly alike when it comes to accepting and trusting a principal who decides to lead with a coach's hat. Preparing your school community to embrace self-exploration through coaching will require planning, effort, and ongoing reflection. This chapter will help you embark on the complex processes of building partnerships, learning to power with rather than power over, explore six partnership principles crucial to every coaching relationship, and collect relationship data.

# Building Partnerships

In the following vignette, Maria, an experienced elementary teacher, describes the qualities shared by the most effective principals she worked with.

### A Teacher's Perspective

I have had about 20 principals throughout my 25-year career as a teacher. When I reflect on the ones who truly made a difference, a few common characteristics emerge.

First of all, they were nonjudgmental. When they gave me suggestions, they did so in a nonthreatening manner, more like a casual conversation:

Principal: Have you ever seen a close reading lesson?
Me: No, what is it?
Principal: It is a strategy that helps kids strengthen comprehension as they read text at deeper levels. I think you'd really love it. Mr. Larsen

has been using it for a while. If you'd like to try it, I'm sure he would be more than happy to let you watch it sometime. Let me know if you're interested.

Rather than making me feel like I was doing something wrong, these principals made me feel like I was missing out on something that I then really wanted to learn more about. I would research the idea a bit and was usually hooked. This allowed me to build a strong repertoire of strategies to help me meet the needs of every learner.

Second, the best principals were also the ones I observed building relationships with the students in the school. They were visible and accessible. They cared about the kids, and the kids loved them, too. Seeing how they interacted with students made me feel like they had my students' best interests at heart and made me want to work harder to be like them and respect what they had to say about teaching and learning.

Third, I had more confidence in the principals who had successful track records as teachers in their chosen fields prior to becoming administrators. It made me feel like they knew what they were talking about, that their advice wasn't just about quoting a textbook they had read while they earned their administrative degree. Anyone can read a textbook, but it takes someone special to be a teacher. If you know the research and best practices but can't implement them in a classroom, then I have a really hard time trusting that what you are telling me is valuable. The best principal I ever had used to say, "I'd love to try the strategy we are currently focusing on; could I borrow your students? Perhaps you can give me some feedback." This showed me that the principal was willing not only to cite the research but also to demonstrate its effectiveness in the classroom.

Finally, the principals who try to make everyone happy are the ones who get the least amount of respect from the teachers. They need to be kind but firm and fair and consistent in the decisions they make.

Maria's assessment of effective principals can be summed up in four adjectives: *nonjudgmental*, *present*, *experienced*, and *consistent*. Like so many teachers with whom we have spoken, she developed respect for principals based on their actions and interactions with teachers and students rather than their words. She respected their visions of education, which were born out of experience and an ongoing connection to teaching and learning, conveyed through concrete examples, and accompanied by a patient openness to her own learning and adaptation of the approaches being championed schoolwide.

We have heard from countless teachers who want to learn and grow with their principals. Many welcome classroom visits and want to be held to high expectations—with a few caveats. They want to feel valued, not afraid of what the principal is going to say about what they do day in and day out. Teaching is an expression of their deepest values, and conversations about teaching touch on their own understanding of themselves. Teachers spend countless hours honing their craft and don't want to be told what to do by someone who is removed from the classroom routine or who does not try to understand their perspectives, fears, and aspirations. They want sincerity, openness, and a lack of hidden agendas. They want to see you learn alongside them to gain an understanding of curricular and student needs. They want partnership.

## Powering With Rather Than Powering Over

The traditional role of principal is one of authority, but that's been changing: as management expert Ken Blanchard has stated, "The key to successful leadership today is influence rather than authority" (quoted in Tucker, 2008, p. 19). Jim Knight, author of *High Impact Instruction* (2013), suggests that principals "commit to modeling *power with* rather than *power over* in all interactions with people (children and adults) in the school" (p. 276).

What does it mean to be a principal leading with *power over*? Let's take a look at the story of Alice, a well-intentioned principal who does not realize how she is being perceived.

### A Principal's Perspective

Alice, a middle school principal, is passionate about education and her school. She refers to teachers and support staff as "hers" with a care and concern that is palpable yet, at times, overwhelming and even domineering. She prides herself on developing well-articulated school improvement plans complete with educational methods that she spends hours researching. She holds high expectations for the staff and teachers, which she clearly expresses at staff meetings.

She states that she has an open door policy and makes herself highly accessible, stopping whatever she might be doing when teachers want to come by to ask a question. Any time a staff member expresses a concern, Alice is quick to offer a solution or address individuals who have been complained about. Yet for some reason that Alice cannot quite discern, the number of staff members coming to speak with her individually has been decreasing over time.

Alice is currently working from a *power over* mindset. By referring to the school and staff as "hers" and solving problems for them rather than asking reflective questions, she is asserting her ownership over others. Her demeanor sets her apart from the rest of the staff. Keeping up-to-date with the latest educational practices is admirable, yet she fails to engage with her staff to understand their hopes, dreams, and visions of teaching and learning and to collaborate with them to develop approaches that value their diverse strengths and perspectives. If she instead sought out coaching for herself and reflected on ways to lead with a coach's hat, Alice would be embracing a *power with* mindset.

## Identifying Your Leadership Style

When it comes to building and nurturing relationships, style matters as much as substance, and adopting an effective leadership style requires tremendous emotional intelligence. It is therefore fitting that Daniel Goleman, who has long championed the notion of emotional intelligence, would have profound insight on leadership styles. In his article "Leadership That Gets Results" (2000), Goleman outlines six essential leadership styles: coercive, authoritative, affiliative, democratic, pacesetting, and coaching. Each of the styles draws on emotional intelligences, although two of them—coercive and pacesetting—have a negative effect. The coercive style is top-down and indicates to employees that their ideas don't matter. Leaders who use the pacesetting style often have good intentions but set high expectations of themselves and others with a demanding attitude. Both of these approaches are antithetical to leading with a coach's hat. Goleman suggests using them only in extreme circumstances and never in isolation.

The remaining four leadership styles—authoritative, affiliative, democratic, and coaching—have a positive effect. Here's a rundown:

- **Authoritative.** An authoritative leader has a developed vision and wants others to follow suit in a manner fitting the individual, allowing them choice. This style is beneficial in schools that need a clear direction; it's not as effective when the leader has less educational experience than the staff.

- **Affiliative.** Leaders who exemplify this style tend to put people first and want to be well liked. They are great at building camaraderie and improving staff morale. The potential downside is that because the focus is on making everyone happy, weaker performance may go uncorrected and staff members may be unclear on the full vision of the school.

- **Democratic.** This leadership style gives everyone a voice, but school climate and morale actually tend to be lower when this is the primary approach. The democratic style often involves endless meetings or open-ended conversation starters that leave employees feeling leaderless and unsure of the organizational focus.

- **Coaching.** The focus of this leadership style is on reflection and self-improvement. Staff members who hold a growth mindset typically embrace this style. Leaders need to be mindful of staff who are hesitant to coaching and ease them into the process.

According to Goleman, the more of these four leadership styles a leader masters, the better. He recommends drawing on the characteristics of each style as needed. Each approach has its benefits and a potential downside, which highlights the need for leaders to be responsive and adaptive, using a mix of approaches and remaining ever-attentive to the needs of those they support. Interestingly, Goleman found coaching to be one of the least commonly used leadership approaches, despite its positive effect, owing to a perceived lack of time and an inadequate understanding of how to lead as a coach. Note that elements of the coaching style outlined in this book appear in all four of the styles Goleman identifies as having a positive effect.

We invite you to spend some time in the coming weeks reflecting on your leadership style. Go about your day as you usually do, but schedule time to reflect on actions and interactions that you can attribute to your leadership style. Figure 3.1 (see p. 58) outlines each of Goleman's four positive leadership styles, reflective questions and areas to consider, and the styles' ties to a coaching mindset. We urge you to record your reflections to help you notice patterns in your leadership style, which will help form your personal blueprint to leading with a coach's hat. You can use the table in Figure 3.2 on page 59 (available as a blank form in the Appendix and online; see note on p. 4) to track these patterns.

Figure 3.1

# Leadership Style Reflection Guide

| Leadership Style | Reflective Questions | Areas to Consider | Ties to a Coaching Mindset |
|---|---|---|---|
| Authoritative | • How do I model being a risk taker and learner?<br><br>• Did I share an overall goal and provide others with their own means to achieve the goal? | How do I exhibit this style with teachers outside the grades and disciplines I have taught? | • Being authoritative doesn't mean telling others what to do. In this context, it is more about empowering others to achieve agreed-upon goals.<br><br>• How have I guided staff to agreed-upon goals? |
| Affiliative | • Am I attempting to build team harmony and morale within the school?<br><br>• How do I use praise?<br><br>• How do I build on strengths? | Does my use of praise allow poor performance to go uncorrected? | As a coach, I can note areas of weakness while looking for strengths. How can I help staff members use their strengths to improve areas of weakness so that poor performance does not go uncorrected? |
| Democratic | How have I allowed for voice and choice in the school? | Does staff show signs of feeling leaderless? | • How can allowing for voice and choice help move the school forward?<br><br>• What is my response when other educators choose an approach that differs from my own belief? |
| Coaching | What type of coaching conversations have I had recently? | How do I address staff resistance to coaching? What other leadership styles can I use to bring these teachers along? | Is the staff aware of my *coach's hat?* How do I overtly distinguish between my work coaching teachers and my evaluation responsibilities? |

Figure 3.2

## Leadership Style Tracker

| Date | Name or Group | Time | Authoritative | Affiliative | Democratic | Coaching |
|------|---------------|------|---------------|-------------|------------|----------|
| 9/4 | Full staff | 9–12 | Modeled myself as a learner by attending PD w/ staff and volunteering to take part in a role-play led by facilitator. | | | |
| 10/28 | Ms. A. | 10–10:30 | | • Noted Ms. A.'s use of student writing in daily journals. We talked about student successes and challenges. I noticed that several opportunities were teacher-directed topics and only read by the teacher. We talked about ways to add authentic audiences. She became interested in looking into student blogging.<br><br>• My intent was to start the conversation with a positive. She was proud of her students' writing. It was evident that they were making progress, yet I hope I pushed her thinking to find ways for more authenticity in both platforms and audience. I will keep following up with her. | | |

Continued

Figure 3.2 *continued*

## Leadership Style Tracker

| Date | Name or Group | Time | Authoritative | Affiliative | Democratic | Coaching |
|---|---|---|---|---|---|---|
| 9/30 | School climate committee | 7:30–8:15 | | | Held first meeting with the school climate committee suggested by staff. Grade-level teams chose their representative. I want to learn from them how to improve overall climate in school as well as how to continue to build trust in my coaching efforts. | |
| 10/28 | Mr. L. | 3:30–4:00 | | | | Had a coaching conversation with Mr. L. today. It was part of his yearly observation, but I took a different approach. I asked him what type of data he'd like me to collect as I was observing. He wanted me to monitor the types of questions he asked during instruction. We agreed that I would write down the questions he asked. At our follow-up meeting today, we looked at his questions. He came to the conclusion that he asked more lower-level questions than he thought. We talked about ways to add more high-level questions. |

Once you have several data points, reflect on the various elements of your current style:

- What do you notice as you review the data?
- Do you have a style that is more dominant than others?
- Is there a style you use with specific groups or in certain situations?
- How could one style lead to the use of another?

Another way to examine your leadership style is to ask yourself a variety of questions that invite you to think about how you see yourself and how others perceive you as a school leader (see Figure 3.3). Looking in the mirror isn't an easy task. Take time to reflect, and be as honest as you can. Try to step outside yourself to understand how you come across to others. Look for evidence to back up your thoughts.

Figure 3.3

## Perceptions Self-Assessment

| How do you perceive yourself? | How do others perceive you? |
| --- | --- |
| How would you describe your relationship with the school staff? How do your actions and conversations build trusting relationships? Do you engage in conversations with a nonjudgmental approach? Do you respect them? What evidence do you have? | How would school staff members describe your relationship with them? Do they trust you? How do they know you respect them? What evidence do you have? |
| How would you describe yourself as a learner? Do you see yourself as the lead expert or the lead learner? In what ways do you model learning along with your staff? How do you share your personal learning with your staff to model yourself as a learner versus an expert? | How would the school staff describe you as a learner? What experiences have staff had to be able to learn along with you? |
| How do you encourage risk taking and a growth mindset in your teachers? How do you and your teachers encourage a growth mindset in your students? How do you respond when a teacher tries something new and it "flops"? How do you support your teachers? | Do teachers feel like they can take risks? Do teachers feel threatened by your presence in their classroom? How do teachers feel supported? |
| How do you show teachers your appreciation? Do you give appreciation to some more than others? | Do teachers feel appreciated for their hard work? Who might not feel appreciated? |

# The Six Partnership Principles

In the quest to adopt a *power with* rather than a *power over* leadership approach, it's helpful to consider techniques used by coaches who deliberately function as partners. Jim Knight, author of *Instructional Coaching: A Partnership Approach to Improving Instruction* (2007), highlights six partnership principles that he views as the aim of every coaching relationship: equality, choice, voice, reflection, dialogue, and praxis. Delving into each of these principles and its potential application will be helpful as you reflect on your own leadership style.

## Equality

The central paradox of leading with a coach's hat is the inherent lack of equality in your relationships with those you supervise. It is therefore essential that you build relationships of mutual respect with your teachers and commit to engaging in ongoing reflection to refine instructional practices.

Principals often talk of being the *lead learners* in a school, and we admire this perspective. The dynamics of education change daily, and staying current by constantly learning is vital. But it is one thing to hone one's craft in isolation and another to learn alongside teachers in a genuine partnership of investigation, discovery, learning, and creativity. When principals and other school leaders function not as experts but, like teachers, as learners who have expertise, a shared sense of wisdom and purpose develops. The process can be quite messy, as educators will sometimes disagree and advocate for different approaches. Yet an open and persuadable leader empowers staff and engages in learning and exploration as an equal even as he or she is ultimately responsible for the vision and direction adopted by the school.

### A Principal's Perspective

Bill was the first to admit that he felt like a fish out of water. Although his teaching experience was at the elementary level, he jumped at the chance to become principal of one of the district's high schools. He realized that he could actually use his lack of high school teaching experience to his advantage and told his teachers early on that he saw his leadership role as that of a learning partner.

Modeling his desire to learn alongside teachers, during his first days on the job he joined the faculty in a training on Socratic seminars that had been scheduled prior to his hire. During the discussion points of the training, Bill asked the teachers at his table questions to help them reflect on their new learning, such as "How do you see this affecting the student learning in your class?" "What challenges do you think may hinder your implementation?" and "What support do you need from me to implement this?" During the lunch and snack breaks, he initiated conversations with teachers, asking about their families, summer travels, and personal interests to build rapport.

As teachers began implementing the new initiative in their classrooms, Bill gave them support to ensure its success. He provided substitute coverage to allow a group of teachers to visit a nearby school that had years of experience with Socratic seminars. He joined them and led a debriefing conversation to empower them to share their findings at the next staff meeting and to brainstorm next steps to ensure that all teachers were continuing to implement what they had learned. When Bill visited classrooms, he provided teachers with feedback specific to their implementation of the new strategies. He covered classes to allow teachers to observe one another, an experience that also added to his understanding of teaching high school students.

As Bill completed the required formal observations and summative evaluations for the district evaluation process, he felt surprisingly comfortable, looking for evidence of all standards easily, with the exception of the content areas with which he did not have expertise. He found himself able to have productive conversations with teachers by asking them reflective questions and letting them do most of the talking.

## Choice

A one-size-fits-all approach isn't beneficial for students *or* teachers. Sure, the goal is for all teachers to learn and reflect on their practices and student learning, but it is counterproductive to force them to do this in only one way. Malcom Shepard Knowles (Knowles, Holton, & Swanson, 2005), known for his study of adult learners, emphasizes that adults (1) need to know why they must learn something, (2) need to learn experientially, (3) approach learning as problem solving, and (4) learn best when the topic is of immediate value. Providing choice honors these principles of adult learning.

Just like students, teachers come with a variety of learning needs and preferences. As principal, you can incorporate the element of choice in a variety of ways:

• Rather than expecting all teachers to attend the same professional learning experiences, think about ways to differentiate, giving them the opportunity to be self-directed learners and choose what fits their specific learning preferences.

• Encourage teachers to set their own learning goals throughout the school year. Engaging in coaching conversations about their students' needs can help them develop these goals. Help teachers see the big picture, but also have them choose ways to break goals down into small wins.

• Allow teachers to be innovative and take risks. Like students, teachers rise to new heights when they are learning in authentic ways. Learning is messy and rarely linear. Talk with them along their journeys and respect their opinions.

### A Principal's Perspective

Linda, an elementary principal with a literacy background, had facilitated a consensus-building process resulting in the study and implementation of The Daily 5 with plans to move into The Literacy

CAFE System the following year. She worked diligently with the building leadership team to provide quality professional learning opportunities for the staff. The team had incorporated collaboration time, something that the staff had requested, to enable teachers to build lessons with their grade-level teams, study student data, and share implementation ideas (Boushey & Moser, 2006, 2009).

Then Linda hit a roadblock with two veteran staff members who were becoming vocally against the idea of implementing the new framework in their classrooms. They had a longstanding, successful history of using a reader's/writer's workshop approach. Linda knew she had to visit with these teachers before matters escalated. Earlier in her administrative career, she had experienced a similar situation when she and staff members hadn't seen eye-to-eye on instructional practices. She hadn't handled that situation well, and as a result principal-teacher trust had been broken. She wanted this time to be different.

She set up a meeting with the two teachers and let them know ahead of time that she wanted to discuss some of the concerns they had expressed at the last staff development session. She didn't want to come across as judgmental; she truly wanted to understand their hesitation. It was a district expectation to implement The Daily 5 as part of its guaranteed and viable curriculum, but perhaps they could find common ground between the teachers' beliefs and the required literacy approaches.

During the meeting, Linda asked the teachers to share more about the reader's/writer's workshop approach they were currently implementing. The teachers' passion for developing lifelong readers was clear. They explained that their current model had resulted in countless student successes and was enabling them to reach their most challenging students. It dawned on Linda that the approaches were more similar than different. She asked if they could chart the similarities and differences together.

As Linda and the teachers continued their visit, the similarities between the approaches became more evident. Linda shared more information about The Literacy CAFE, and the teachers became quite interested in what was coming the following year. Linda agreed to purchase both of them the book and told them that she wanted to know their thoughts on it. All three left the meeting with a better understanding of one another's visions and intentions.

## Voice

We all feel valued and respected when our voices, ideas, thoughts, and opinions matter. One way to create an environment open to teacher voice is to be genuinely curious. Think about any 3-year-old you've encountered: the question *Why?* is probably one of his or her favorite utterances. Principals who want to lead with a coach's hat can learn a lot from the curiosity of a 3-year-old. You don't need to sound like a broken record constantly asking "Why?", but you can concentrate on talking less, listening more, and asking questions that you don't already have the answers to.

Albert Einstein is quoted as having said, "I have no special talent. I am only passionately curious." Einstein's curiosity touched the future. The concepts he discovered decades ago continue to be the basis of current-day inventions. Teachers are charged with touching the future daily. Ask just about any educator why he or she became a teacher, and the response is typically "to make a difference in the lives of children." The same holds true for administrators: we are in the business of affecting lives, building futures, and inspiring greatness.

Still, eliciting teacher voice can be easier said than done. Many teachers need to trust their principals' motives before truly opening up. The way you phrase questions matters. If you sound like you're interrogating teachers or asking "gotcha" questions, trust can be diminished. One effortless coaching prompt that can yield thoughtful reflection is "Tell me more about that." Try also replacing "why" questions—which can put people on the defensive—with "what" or "how" questions.

Imagine you just ate a delicious piece of pizza. If someone asked, "Why did you eat that?" you may immediately assume that eating the pizza was something you should not have done. You'd focus more on defending your actions than on considering the question. If instead someone asked, "How did you choose what to eat?" or "What led to your decision to try the pizza?" you would feel more inclined simply to explain your decision. Keep in mind that even this wording may put some teachers on the defensive. It can take time for them to realize that you are not trying to "get" them but, rather, merely opening a conversation with some reflective questions.

Even more important than how you phrase questions or prompts is finding elements in a teacher's repertoire that you are honestly curious about. You may find it helpful to practice being curious outside your educational comfort zone. Say you're a former 5th grade teacher who implemented highly effective literacy practices and whose students excelled. The 5th grade teacher at your school is probably aware of your record and may feel threatened if you start asking her questions, even if you are truly intrigued by something you observed during her reading instruction. Instead, head down to the kindergarten classroom. What do you see? What do you want to know more about—not with the intention of trying to change something, but with the aim of understanding and supporting teachers to reflect on their work? What are the students doing that simply amazes you? Would a simple conversation with the teacher provide an opportunity for him or her to feel more empowered as an educator?

Teachers often go through their days unaware of their own influence on students. Making the time to discuss something you are eager to learn about from them shows that you appreciate their efforts. The interaction may also lead them to be more tuned in to what they or their students are doing in the classroom.

Many schools we have visited and worked with have well-developed building leadership teams in place. The teams usually consist of representatives from each grade level or department who serve as the voice of their colleagues. The following vignette looks at how one principal created a leadership team to increase teachers' voice in school decision making.

### A Principal's Perspective

Anne was a veteran principal who had received a variety of leadership awards throughout her career. She was well liked and approachable. While studying the concept of balanced leadership, she decided to change her leadership style from that of a manager to that of a leader who valued teacher voice.

After assembling a building leadership team composed of representatives from each grade level in her elementary school, she and the team members identified students' math performance as a particular area of concern. Upon examination of teacher practices, the team determined that math approaches in the school were all over the board, despite the district's set math program. Realizing that math instruction needed to be more consistent within and across grade levels, the grade-level representatives on the leadership team gathered ideas from their grade-level teams. Teachers at every grade level mentioned using guided practice as part of math instruction, so, with the full staff's consensus, the building leadership team set out to study the approach through books, videos, and the help of an outside consultant.

After they felt comfortable with the approach, the members of the leadership team began implementing it in their classrooms, believing that it was important to pilot the approach before bringing the full staff on board. Team members partnered up and worked together to implement and coach each other through the approach.

As the school year came to a close, the team shared its results with the entire staff. It was decided that the team would begin training the rest of the staff on the approach the following year. Teachers were excited by the opportunity to learn more about this approach, since they had already heard great things from their colleagues about the results they saw.

Anne was amazed by the difference that listening to teacher voice had made in pursuing school improvement. She admitted that she had been fearful at first, assuming that "teacher voice" equaled letting teachers do whatever they wanted. The difference came when she and the team considered the needs of students and the ideas generated from the staff. Actually working with and listening to teachers not only helped her gain staff buy-in more quickly but also gave her a better understanding of what staff needed in terms of learning, time, and resources. Teachers appreciated that she walked the walk. Come the following fall, Anne was better equipped to lead with a coach's hat and felt confident facilitating learning and reflective dialogue along with the building leadership team.

## Reflection

One of the greatest gifts of working with a coach is getting the chance to truly reflect. Like guided reading groups in which the teacher supports students to read just above their independent reading level, guided exploration with coaches represents perhaps the most powerful venue in which to stretch our thinking and our skills. We do so not through instruction but through reflection.

According to Pete Hall and colleagues in *The Principal Influence*, "The more reflective we are, the more effective we are" (Hall, Childs-Bowen, Cunningham-Morris, Pajardo, & Simeral, 2016, p. 92). Principals who lead with a coach's hat model genuine reflective thinking and nurture it by listening and asking probing questions that lead to self-discovery.

Principals' greatest challenges to supporting reflection are the intense pace of their days and the huge demands placed upon them. We all show our greatest weaknesses when we are feeling pressured, stressed, and tired. During such times, despite being fully engaged by the requirements of their job, principals are paradoxically not fully present, instead finding themselves occupied with the plans in their heads and the tasks to be accomplished.

They are busy for good reason: the stakes are high, and their own sense of responsibility compels them at times to behave with an intensity that can be unhealthy. In the book *Unmistakable Impact* (2011), Jim Knight quotes a learning leader from one of his institutes expressing a perspective to which we can relate:

> We can't wait. Our kids need to do better today. We can't wait to be nice to teachers. We can't do all this touchy-feely listening stuff. Our teachers need to get better now. Or they need to be gone. Because our kids deserve better. (p. 20)

We've been there: weighted by intense pressure from educational reformers, supervisors, parents, and other stakeholders to improve instruction and give children the education they deserve. And we've learned that demanding immediate improvement without giving educators the opportunity to delve deep into practice through thoughtful reflection and collaborative planning simply does not work.

### A Principal's Perspective

John, a middle school principal determined to create a school of excellence that was good enough for his own children, often felt the same way as the leader quoted above. During his years as an administrator, he had tended to be autocratic, handing down improvement plans, letters of direction, and even formal discipline. Over time, however, he learned that when he stepped back and entered conversations with the sole intent of giving teachers time to reflect instead of just telling them to improve, he—and they—made much better progress.

## Dialogue

Many districts' evaluation systems require teachers to create student outcome goals (also known as student learning outcomes, student learning goals, or professional practice goals) at the beginning of the year. Setting up individual meetings with teachers to discuss these goals also provides a great opportunity to start developing trusting relationships (see Chapter 4 for more on the goal-setting process).

Although teachers may not initially view the meetings as anything more than a mandatory hoop to jump through, you can develop dialogue methods that allow for more teacher reflection and less "principal talk," transforming these meetings into valuable opportunities for professional growth and relationship building. Engaging in these conversations with curiosity and empathy encourages educators to find their voice and articulate their own core values and visions as teachers, learners, and individuals. Their visions may not entirely align with yours, but these open, collaborative conversations often enable you to determine a plan that you both feel enthusiastic about.

Most districts mandate midyear and end-of-year check-ins on these student outcome goals; we suggest you take it one step further by adding additional meeting times to your calendar. Although most principals fully intend to meet with teachers on a regular basis, unless they create a specific plan to do so, check-ins may be sporadic or irregularly distributed among teachers. By intentionally setting up a schedule at the start of the year and sharing it with your staff, you will be more likely to stick with it, and teachers won't be wondering, "Why did he just come in here?"

At the beginning of each meeting, we suggest asking a general question like "How is everything going?" Showing genuine interest in what teachers have to say about their upcoming vacations, their children's recent milestones, or even personal battles such as health issues or a divorce can go miles toward building strong relationships.

Once you've warmed up, ask questions about teachers' goals, student progress, or new strategies the teachers are working on. Your role is to ask questions, listen, and help teachers identify what they're going to do next and how you can help. The support teachers need may be as mundane as getting extra chairs to accommodate a larger class or as substantive as having you cover a class so that they can observe strategies being implemented in another classroom. Provide teachers with any follow-up feedback that you may have from your classroom visits. Make sure to recognize their efforts and progress, and record your notes after each meeting so that you can observe teachers' new learning in action during your next classroom visits.

### A Principal's Perspective

Steve was in his third year as principal at a highly diverse inner-city middle school. Student test scores were poor, and he was under pressure from the district office to turn things around. He had never worked in an environment with such a pronounced lack of trust among staff members; teachers at the school worked in isolation and often had negative attitudes. Although he had been successful in previous schools, he was unsure of what to do here. He knew the school was in dire need of change and feared that he would soon be transferred or asked to leave.

Steve decided that he needed to meet with teachers individually, but first he sent out a simple anonymous staff survey asking three questions:

—What are your hopes for your students?

—What are your hopes for our school?

—How best can we work together as a staff to achieve your hopes for your students and for our school?

Looking for patterns, Steve categorized the responses to each question. When he had tabulated the results, he couldn't believe his eyes: the seemingly negative staff that worked in isolation held incredibly similar hopes for both students and the school as a whole.

He shared these data with the staff, and together they began to develop strategies for transforming their hopes into achievable goals. He then met with teachers individually to set personal short-term goals, asking,

—What are your strengths as a teacher?

—What are your challenges as a teacher?

—As you think about your strengths and challenges and our hopes for our school, what short-term goal would you like to set for yourself?

—How can I support you in meeting this goal?

—How could fellow staff members support you in meeting this goal?

At the close of each meeting, Steve said that he looked forward to supporting the teacher to reach his or her professional best. After his subsequent classroom visits, he made a point to provide teachers with feedback specific to the individual goals they had set. Listening to teachers instead of assuming he knew how they felt, guiding them to the realization that they all had similar hopes for their students and the school as a whole, and helping them identify concrete steps to achieve their hopes shifted their focus from the challenges they faced to an embrace of their capabilities.

### Praxis

Praxis is the exercise or practice of an art, a science, or a skill—or, as we think of it, *walking the talk*. We like the metaphor Dave Burgess, author of *Teach Like a Pirate* (2012), uses when he asks, "Are you a lifeguard or a swimmer?" As he explains, "Lifeguards sit above the action and supervise the pool. Although he or she is focused, there is a distinct sense of separateness both physically and mentally. In contrast, a swimmer is out participating and an integral part of the action" (pp. 14–15). Wearing a coach's hat means getting in the water. Being a lifeguard isn't bad; we all need lifeguards in our lives. But principal-coaches take on the roles of a lifeguard *and* a swimmer, fully immersing themselves both in their own work and in the work of their staffs. Figure 3.4 (see p. 74) provides a side-by-side look at the two roles; which one do you think you embody in your praxis?

# Gathering Relationship Data

Instructional coaches often help teachers collect data in a variety of areas to help them gain insight on their practice, including student engagement, the quality and tone of student-teacher interactions, the types of questions asked by the teacher during a class period, and so on. These data help teachers put their current practice in perspective and get an idea of where they may want to set goals. Once they are working to meet their goals, they can continue to collect data to compare against the baseline data collected at the outset.

Figure 3.4

## Are You a Lifeguard or a Swimmer?

| Administrators as Lifeguards . . . | Administrators as Swimmers . . . |
|---|---|
| • Attend professional development with teachers but may sit toward the back and interact only with fellow administrators. | • Fully engage in professional learning and dialogue with a variety of teachers. |
| • Tell teachers to implement new approaches and initiatives by a specific date. | • Learn and implement new approaches and initiatives alongside teachers, trying them out with students, reflecting on the learning process, and continually adjusting strategies and improving skills. |
| • Make observations in classrooms followed by top-down or closed-ended feedback (e.g., "I like how you engaged students in the close reading approach that we are studying as a staff."). | • Make observations in classrooms followed by reflective feedback and questioning (e.g., "I noticed how you engaged students in the close reading approach that we are studying as a staff. How did you go about determining the focus of your lesson?"). |
| • Use summative data as the measure of success for students and teachers. | • Engage the entire staff in ongoing dialogue about the existing data that most accurately reflect student learning as well as any gaps that need to be filled and develop a data wall with teachers to show changes and areas of concern for students. |
| • Develop schedules for interventions to take place in school. | • Develop schedules as well as assist with interventions and may be responsible for a small group of students. |
| • Read professional material, subscribe to educational journals, and stay current in the field of education. | • Read professional material, subscribe to educational journals, stay current in the field of education, and interact with others at the school level and globally via social media to gain a deeper understanding of education from a variety of perspectives. |
| • Monitor various areas of school such as hallways, lunchrooms, and playgrounds to ensure that all is safe and orderly. | • Monitor areas of the school to ensure that all is safe and orderly and interact with students by greeting them by name as they enter the school, talking with them in the lunchroom, and joining in on playground activities. |

Principals who lead with a coach's hat also strive to collect a variety of data points to help them reflect on their practice and the status of teaching and learning in their schools. Collecting your own data is a valuable way to monitor your journey toward becoming a principal-coach. So far in this chapter, you have had the chance to reflect on your leadership style and gain a better understanding of coaching relationships. Now we invite you to begin gathering relationship data by studying your interactions with staff. Feel free to collect and study these data by yourself or with a trusted colleague in your district or beyond.

We divide principal-teacher interactions into three categories: coaching, management, and evaluative. Feel free to add other categories that describe the day-to-day interactions you experience in your specific role. Here's a rundown of the three categories we're focusing on here.

In coaching interactions, principals

- Work as equals with staff, valuing others' expertise.
- Offer staff choice.
- Allow all voices to be heard.
- Provide opportunities for reflection.
- Engage in meaningful dialogue with staff.
- Walk the talk.

In management interactions, principals

- Maintain a safe environment for staff and students.
- Oversee daily operations of the building.
- Deal with student discipline issues.
- Meet with parents, central office staff, and community members.
- Serve on district committees.
- Write schedules.

In evaluative interactions, principals

- Conduct district-required teacher evaluations.
- Address and document performance concerns with staff.

Set a time frame you are comfortable with—perhaps a few days to a week—and go about your regular routine. Do not try to change your interaction style; you are merely collecting baseline data. After an interaction with a staff member or group, simply jot down the name or group, the date and time, the type of interaction, and a few notes to help you remember the interaction. Some principals carry a small notepad with them daily or use an electronic application such as Evernote. This note taking isn't meant to take up too much of your time. You can make a few notes and then transfer them to a form like the one shown in Figure 3.5 (available as a blank form in the Appendix and online; see note on p. 4) to analyze at a later date.

Figure 3.5

## Interactions Tracker

| Date | Name or Group | Time | Coaching | Management | Evaluative | Notes |
|------|---------------|------|----------|------------|------------|-------|
| 9/4 | Miss A. | 12:30 | X | | | Talked with teacher after informal classroom visit. Asked a few clarifying questions. |
| 9/11 | Mrs. B. | 2:40 | | X | | Teacher sent student to office for disciplinary reasons. |
| 9/20 | Mr. C. | 10:20 | | | X | Conducted a classroom observation tied to yearly evaluation of teacher. |

After you have collected a set of data, take time to analyze it:

• What is your ratio of coaching to management to evaluative interactions?

• What patterns do you notice? With specific teachers? At certain times?

- What type of interaction is taking up most of your time?
- Are there management or evaluative interactions that could shift to coaching interactions with a few minor adjustments?

No two sets of interaction data will be alike, just as no two days in the life of a principal are alike. Taking the time to study your interaction patterns will provide you with a starting point. As you continue reading this book, refer back to both these interaction data and the leadership style data you collected. You may not know how to adjust your interaction or leadership style right now, but the remainder of this book will provide the adjustments and support you need to lead with a coach's hat.

## *HAT*: Remembering the Key Relationship Elements

The education field is notorious for its acronyms, and we are about to add another to your list: *HAT*. We came up with this mnemonic to help you remember the coaching mindset needed to empower and influence others.

*H* stands for *humility*. Yes, your position gives you the highest authority in the building, and you hold more degrees than some of the staff, but education is a people business. Theodore Roosevelt's oft-cited quote "No one cares how much you know until they know how much you care" still holds true today. Find ways to show you appreciate staff members. Get to know them, and let them get to know you! Most important, keep in mind that you are not superhuman. Today's school leaders are often expected to do more than they are humanly capable of doing, but you aren't going to be able to please everyone all the time. When you end up taking on or promising more than you can uphold, your relationships will suffer. Be humble in knowing that you are just one person. Shifting from a *power over* to a *power with* mindset will help: together, you really are better. You don't need to have all the answers; the answers are found within your school.

*A* stands for *action*. Principals are respected when they walk the talk and act with integrity. To gain acceptance in a coaching environment, you need to model action, even when something is out of your comfort zone. If you want teachers and students to take risks, you need to do the same. To truly understand what it is like to be coached, it's important to accept being coached yourself. Is there another school leader in your district who could serve as your coach? Could you reach out to someone else in your surrounding area or state? We know many principals who have connected with other administrators via social media outlets such as Twitter (some useful hashtags include #educoach and #principalpln, or #coachapproach to discuss this book) and even meet and coach one another through virtual communication tools such as Skype, Google Hangouts, FaceTime, or Voxer. Discovering firsthand the empowerment that coaching brings will provide you with valuable insight and skills for coaching others. Be open with the school staff about what you are gaining from having a coach of your own. Share your moments of growth as well as your challenges. If they see you benefit and grow as an educator through coaching, they may be more open to being coached themselves.

Finally, *T* stands for *trust*. First, trust the process of acquiring a coach's hat. This trust is part of the process of adding coaching skills to your repertoire. Think about the leadership style and interaction data you collected throughout this chapter. Accept where you are now and continue to set goals for yourself throughout your journey.

Second, continue to build trusting relationships with the staff. Teachers will need to trust that coaching is a different process from the typical, obligatory evaluation that principals conduct. We urge you to develop the coaching process *with* teachers rather than just announcing that you will now be "coaching them." Learn to navigate between your coaching role and the other aspects of your position. Trust will also come with transparency, so share your intentions with your superintendent as well as teacher union representatives. No one should be surprised when you put on your coach's hat.

# Conclusion

Among the most meaningful relationships a person can have is one with a capable coach who is entirely invested in her or his success. Helping teachers to find the best within themselves requires principal-coaches to create an environment in which teachers can experience both vulnerability and possibility. Although instructional coaching is in itself profoundly challenging, embracing the coach approach as a school leader is exponentially more complex, as the leader balances the demands of being a supervisor with the potential of functioning as a coach. The relationships such leaders develop require them to seek ways to explore the possible, avoiding the temptation to guide teachers to predetermined perspectives and instead opening themselves to discover with teachers new questions and creative solutions that neither teacher nor principal-coach could have imagined alone.

## Put On Your Coach's Hat

*Reflect on your practice:*

- Think of times when you have led with a *power with* mindset. How did staff respond?

- Are there instances when you lead with a *power over* mindset? How might you incorporate a *power with* mindset in these cases?

- After using the Leadership Style Tracker in Figure 3.2, what did you learn about your leadership style? Is there a style that is more dominant than others?

- As you interact with teachers, how do your questions and comments encourage them to reflect on their practice?

- After reviewing Figure 3.4, do you see yourself more as a lifeguard or a swimmer? How do you think your staff would respond to that question? What practices can you change to become a swimmer more of the time?

*Continued*

• Use Figure 3.5 to reflect on your interactions with staff. What categories do most of your interactions fall into? Would you like to increase your number of coaching interactions? If so, what would you like to change?

*Next steps:*
• Use the Leadership Style Tracker or the Interactions Tracker throughout your day for the next couple of weeks to gather information on how you are leading and interacting with your staff.
• Based on your reflections on these data, set a goal to help you move forward with your coach's hat.
• Find a colleague in your school or district or through social media with whom you feel comfortable sharing your goal. The more opportunities you have to reflect on and converse about this goal, the more likely you are to follow through.

––––––– Four –––––––

# Giving Feedback to Increase Effectiveness

*The term* feedback *is often used to describe all kinds of comments made after the fact, including advice, praise, and evaluation. But none of these are feedback, strictly speaking. . . . Basically, feedback is information about how we are doing in our efforts to reach a goal.*

—Grant Wiggins

As much as we appreciate receiving feedback, we often notice a tightness in our shoulders, an acceleration of our heartbeat, or a fluttering in our stomach as we await reactions to our work. We long for critique to help us improve, but we simultaneously hope for praise—and then we feel embarrassed by our yearning for a pat on the back. We want to learn, stretch our thinking, improve our practice; yet we also feel insecure and crave reassurance and affirmation.

When we offer feedback to teachers, we often sense similar feelings: a mix of anxiety, hope, unease, ambivalence, curiosity, embarrassment, and anticipation. These conversations tend to feel awkward, especially with teachers who are unused to receiving nonevaluative feedback.

The reason for this ambivalence is that for most of our lives, as students and as professionals, we have not actually received feedback. We have not been offered, in the words of Grant Wiggins (2012), "information about how we are doing in our efforts to reach a goal." Instead, we have received "all kinds of comments made after the fact, including advice, praise, and evaluation," none of which "are feedback, strictly speaking" (p. 11).

John Hattie (2009) found that feedback is one of the top 10 influences on student achievement. Yet he offers a strong caution: feedback is also among the most *variable* factors. In other words, the quality of feedback is fundamental. The key to giving effective feedback, according to Hattie, is the ability to reflect on progress toward transparent, challenging goals connected to clear success criteria. Although Hattie's research describes the effect of teacher-student feedback, he asserts that the research findings pertain to professional learning as well.

## What Feedback is *Not*: Advice, Praise, and Evaluation

As we have sought to transform our leadership by incorporating more coaching, we have seen our relationships with family members, friends, and colleagues transform as well. In the past, when people in our lives— our children, spouses, siblings, friends, colleagues, teachers we supervise, and others—came to us to talk about a challenging or confusing situation they were dealing with, we implicitly assumed that they were seeking advice, praise, or an evaluation of their actions. We readily complied—not necessarily with what they actually sought, but with what we perceived they sought. Sometimes they appreciated the advice, praise, or evaluative judgment we so readily offered; other times they politely ignored it; and still other times they rejected it, at times even angrily.

In time, as we embraced the potential of nonjudgmental observation and reflection, we found ourselves listening more carefully, asking more open-ended questions, and holding back on offering opinions. We still grapple with finding a balance between advice, praise, or evaluative opinions and nonjudgmental coaching feedback. Yet far more often than in the past, we recognize ourselves not primarily as advisers, cheerleaders, or judges but, rather, as coaches invested in helping others to articulate goals and to decide how to go about achieving those goals.

## On Advice

A coaching mindset requires deep humility and genuine curiosity. Although there are times when advice is warranted, when it is offered too quickly or too frequently, it can easily undermine coaching efforts. Teachers who rely on leaders to provide the answers (and sometimes even the questions) are not empowered to set and navigate their own course toward ambitious goals.

An experience that can jolt principals out of adviser mode is visiting the classroom of a teacher in an unfamiliar discipline or grade; one of our favorite choices is a foreign language class taught exclusively in a language that the principal does not speak. The visitor may be surprised to find that in unfamiliar territory he or she is still able to identify and observe familiar components: classroom management, the learning environment, active student engagement, formative assessment, and more. Wearing the coach's hat in an area in which you are a novice can be a powerful learning experience, helping you gain skill in offering nonjudgmental feedback rather than advice.

### A Principal's Perspective

Mr. Simmons is a former school guidance counselor who took on the role of elementary principal without any experience as a teacher or an instructional coach. He had taught character education and social skills classes and had logged time in many different classrooms, yet he lacked formal teacher training. Capitalizing on his own distinct perspective, he often jokes with teachers that they are lucky he's not an expert, as that frees him to view them as the experts they truly are. He spends time in classrooms observing what teachers are doing, asks questions to further his learning, and solicits teachers' input on what they want him to look for when he conducts formal observations.

Mr. Simmons gives his teachers ownership over their teaching and professional learning, and he honors the work they are doing. He uses what he learns from his strongest teachers to support struggling teachers. He has come to believe that his unique background has been extremely beneficial, enabling him to support teachers with a coaching mindset. He has likened his approach to that of a counselor, who does not give advice but instead helps people to find their own solutions. "The principal can't be an expert in everything," Mr. Simmons explains, "so I go to my experts and learn from them. If I were to try to portray myself as an expert, I would lose my teachers' trust. Instead, I empower them to be the experts." His words are a vital reminder to all who seek to lead schools with a coach's hat, regardless of their levels or areas of expertise and experience.

## On Praise

Whereas refraining from giving advice when we offer feedback has required practice, refraining from giving *praise* while offering feedback has challenged our fundamental notions of what it means to lead. Central to our perspectives on leadership and coaching is the importance of showing appreciation, focusing on the positive, and celebrating success. We deeply respect the work of our teachers and believe they deserve praise.

Make no mistake about it: praise plays an important role in a positive school culture. Author Hal Urban (2012) relayed in a conference keynote address that during his first four years of teaching, he received only constructive criticism during conferences with his principal and department chair—no compliments on what he was doing well. Although he appreciated their insight into what he could do to improve, the lack of praise drained his morale. Urban, like so many other teachers, was not receiving feedback at all: he was receiving advice and evaluation, but without the praise.

The key to incorporating praise is to avoid confusing it with feedback. Hattie (2009) unequivocally recommends separating feedback from praise, which dissipates the positive effect of feedback. Effective principal-coaches show how much they value staff by offering both praise and non-judgmental feedback to help teachers set and achieve ambitious goals; they are just careful not to offer praise and feedback at the same time. This realization has been vital to our work in determining how to lead with a coach's hat.

Although praise offered in concert with feedback undermines the effect of the feedback, an appreciative culture is a necessary backdrop to any efforts to promote high productivity and achievement. Marcial Losada and Emily Heaphy (2004) ranked 60 business teams in terms of performance, as measured by profit and loss statements, customer satisfaction surveys, and 360 reviews by superiors, peers, and subordinates. Analyzing the team conversations, they found that high-performing teams had an average ratio of positive to negative interactions of 5.8 to 1. Average-performing teams were only slightly more positive than negative, with a ratio of 1.8 to 1, and low-performing teams had an average positive-to-negative ratio of 1 to 20. Similarly, in *How Full Is Your Bucket?* Tom Rath and Donald Clifton (2004) cite a study finding that workgroups that had ratios of more than three positive interactions for every negative interaction were significantly more productive than were teams that did not reach this ratio. Interestingly, the study revealed that productivity also declines when the positive-to-negative ratio goes higher than 13 positive interactions for every negative interaction. Balance is essential.

When leaders work to nurture an appreciative culture in which feedback can thrive, they resemble the "yard guy" in Jon Gordon's *The No Complaining Rule: Positive Ways to Deal with Negativity at Work* (2008). The yard guy uses an organic mixture that "creates an environment where the good grass can grow healthy and strong" (p. 64) to the point where the weeds are crowded out. Similarly, principal-coaches commit themselves to creating the conditions necessary for highly effective teaching and learning, which spread to the point that negative attitudes and practices are crowded out. These conditions involve, among many other activities, demonstrating appreciation. Explicit written appreciation, as well as verbal appreciation, is often far more valued than principals recognize.

### A Principal's Perspective

Before the iPad became Rob's tool of choice for sending feedback to teachers, he used to leave handwritten notes in teachers' mailboxes expressing appreciation. One day over the summer, as he was searching a classroom for a teaching book, Rob came across an assemblage of notes taped to the inside of a cupboard door. Not one to nose around his teachers' classrooms, he nonetheless took a long enough look to see that this teacher had kept all of his positive notes over the years.

Although Rob finds the iPad a convenient tool to use during classroom visits, he doesn't think e-mails pack the same punch as those handwritten notes. Since his discovery, he has made a concerted effort to give each of his teachers at least one handwritten appreciative note at some point during the school year.

## On Evaluation

In distinguishing feedback and evaluation, we arrive at the heart of the challenge of being a principal-coach. You cannot lead with a coach's hat without struggling to reconcile the contradictory tasks of evaluating and coaching. By using the metaphor of the "evaluator's hat" and the "coach's hat," we have achieved an admittedly uncomfortable balance, evaluating when we are required to while continuously offering nonjudgmental feedback to help teachers reflect on their progress toward professional goals. Balancing these roles isn't easy, and it is particularly charged in our current climate of standardized teacher effectiveness initiatives. Some districts' evaluation systems include observation forms with checklists requiring principals to actively look for deficits, which leaves teachers feeling like they're being examined under a microscope, their imperfections amplified and their teaching choices misunderstood and critiqued out of context. Putting on the coach's hat as much as possible during formal evaluations has the potential to transform the process.

### A Principal's Perspective

For several years, Nathan made sure to complete each teacher's evaluation before meeting with the teacher for the post-observation conference. By the time they met, he had already rated the teacher based on his formal observation and the evidence he had collected. It took Nathan years to realize that his conversations with teachers were one-sided: he was doing all of the talking.

The catalyst for change was a formal observation he conducted in Mrs. Minton's classroom. On that day, he noticed that one of Mrs. Minton's students was completely disengaged, keeping her head down and drawing in a notebook the entire lesson, never looking up. Nathan waited for Mrs. Minton—an outstanding teacher—to use engagement strategies he'd seen her use before, such as proximity, think-pair-share, or written response. But to his surprise, she did nothing to engage the student.

During their post-observation conference at the end of the day, Mrs. Minton confided to Nathan how worried she was about this student. That morning, the student had told her about a big fight her parents had had the night before. The student had seen her dad arrested, and she and her mom were staying in a shelter. The school counselor was out that day, so Mrs. Minton did her best to provide support by letting this student talk with her during recess and giving her a notebook to draw and write in to try to make it through the day.

This was the day Nathan's written evaluation practices changed. He realized that if he had not had a conversation with Mrs. Minton before completing her written evaluation, she would have earned a "needs improvement" rating in the area of student engagement. However, through their conversation, he learned that contrary to appearances, Mrs. Minton had not been ignoring a disengaged student; she had been providing a safe harbor for a child in crisis.

Once Nathan started wearing his coach's hat during conversations with teachers, the entire evaluative process was transformed. He asked reflective questions. Teachers did more of the talking and came up with their own professional goals. He supported them in working toward these goals, and teachers continued to grow.

As coaches fully invested in our teachers' success, we want to be able to differentiate and adapt our evaluation approaches to support the wide range of learning preferences, interests, and needs our teachers present. We wish we could forgo standardized, deficit-based evaluations altogether and instead engage in a robust process of goal setting followed by feedback and reflection. Given that districts require formal evaluations, however, we do our best to transform these evaluations into opportunities for meaningful professional learning and growth. The following tips will help you do so, too.

• Before the school year starts, create a yearlong schedule spacing out the formal observations month by month, and distribute copies to all teachers. When creating this schedule, plan fewer observations during the busiest times of the year and more observations during slower times of the year. Make sure to include a statement reading something like "Please do not stress about your formal observation. By the time I am in your room for an entire lesson, I will already have done several class visits and seen you 'in action.' This is an opportunity for me to observe an entire lesson and for us to engage in reflective dialogue for professional growth."

• When scheduling an observation, schedule the pre- and post-conference all at once. If possible, schedule the post-conference on the same day as the formal observation, remembering that the conversation with the teacher is the most important part of this process.

- Give all teachers a pre-conference form ahead of time so that they know what questions to be prepared to discuss during your meeting. Here are some of the types of questions we recommend:
    1. What are the objectives or desired outcomes for this lesson?
    2. Describe the population of the class and how you've planned to differentiate this lesson. [*Note*: once you know teachers' classes well from frequent class visits, you will no longer need to ask about the population.]
    3. What will I be observing? What instructional methods will you be using?
    4. How will you assess student performance throughout or after the lesson? What evidence of success or achievement are you looking for?
    5. Is there anything particular that you would like me to observe during the lesson and provide specific feedback on?
    6. What do you believe to be any areas of concern?

- Complete as much of the observation form as you can while you are observing in the classroom, but jot down follow-up questions you'd like to ask the teacher in the post-conference and wait to finish the form until after you have had the post-observation discussion.

## Goal Setting

We've established that feedback is "information about how we are doing in our efforts to reach a goal." It follows, then, that when there are no goals, there is no feedback. You can diligently spend time, fully present, in classrooms. You can hone your listening skills and offer a safe space for teachers to reflect. Yet if you and your teachers do not set goals, there is no possible way you can monitor progress, celebrate success, or identify obstacles. Goal setting is core to leading with a coach's hat.

Goal setting for others and ourselves can be excruciating, exhilarating, and everything in between, depending on the particular experiences of teachers, coaches, and the communities they serve together. Goal setting entails vulnerability, as we acknowledge a gap between where we are and where we aspire to be. It also entails hopeful embrace of our own potential to improve, accomplish, and succeed. For us, setting goals is an energizing process that helps us to understand more deeply some of the values, fears, aspirations, and ideals of the teachers with whom we work.

We've grappled with setting our own transparent and challenging goals with clear success criteria, just as we have patiently supported teachers to come up with their own. In the process, we've found that we need to be sensitive to some teachers' tendency to base their goals on what they *think* we want. This habit demonstrates years of conditioning that many educators have experienced, both as students and as teachers, to try to please those in positions of authority—and, in the process, abdicate ownership of their own learning. As principal-coaches, we aim to empower teachers to direct their own professional learning, setting goals relevant to them and their students.

We begin by setting our own goals and sharing them with faculty. Afterward, we meet individually with all the educators we supervise—teachers as well as administrators—to support them in coming up with a professional learning goal, an action plan for meeting the goal, supports to use throughout the process, and evidence we will use to monitor progress. Our only requirement for the goals is that they are closely connected to improving quality of learning or community for students.

Here are some examples of goals chosen by teachers we've worked with:

• Develop a broader, more nuanced approach to assessing student learning and use those assessment results to plan ongoing instruction.

• Create a learning environment in which all students participate actively in both full-class and collaborative small-group activities.

- Gain greater skill in designing differentiated learning experiences for collaborative and independent student learning.
- Strengthen relationships with parents both through technology and by making connections face-to-face.
- Develop greater comfort and skill in teaching math, including differentiating instruction for students at a higher level of mastery.
- Collaborate in a serious way with members of the grade-level team to support student learning.
- Use time as effectively as possible to enable students to engage in the types of learning they need to be successful.
- More effectively use the SMART Board as an interactive learning tool.
- Incorporate higher-order thinking when questioning students.

Let's take a closer look at how two of the professional learning goals listed above were actualized, including action steps, supports, and evidence of progress.

**Example 1**

---

*Goal:* Incorporate higher-order thinking when questioning students.

*Action steps:*

- During lesson preparation, plan questions that require students to engage in higher-order thinking.
- During teaching, reflect on possible follow-up higher-order thinking questions to ask based on student responses.
- Deliberately plan a range of questions for different learners; think about questions to ask particular students.
- Note which students are able to answer higher-order thinking questions.
- Strive to stretch each student from where he or she currently is.
- Provide wait time after asking questions.

---

*Continued*

| Supports: |
| --- |
| Mentoring provided by a colleague who has been trained in mentoring new teachers. |

| Evidence of progress toward goal: |
| --- |
| • Notes on questions asked and student answers given; evidence in those notes of student growth over time.<br>• Collection of evidence by the mentor, who observes a lesson and uses a form to keep track of the questions asked, wait time, student responses, and other components. |

## Example 2

| Goal: Use time as effectively as possible to enable students to engage in the types of learning they need to be successful. |
| --- |
| **Action steps:** |
| • Identify strategies with which to reduce loss of teaching time owing to interruptions, inefficient transitions, and ineffective classroom routines and structures.<br>• Prioritize learning goals for students and deliberately allocate sufficient time for high priorities.<br>• Use a written schedule posted for students and a timer to stay on schedule each day.<br>• Organize student time and materials more efficiently (e.g., have assignments ready on students' desks when they come into the classroom). |
| **Supports:** |
| • Membership in a professional association that can provide helpful resources, such as Learning Forward or ASCD.<br>• Peer coaching to help collect data on time spent on and off task. |
| **Evidence of progress toward goal:** |
| • Documentation of planning and written reflection on whether plans went as anticipated.<br>• Regular written reflection on use of time that provides evidence of gaining greater skill in using time effectively. |

Teachers may struggle to determine their own goals for a variety of reasons. Some teachers initially choose goals so broad as to be meaningless, while others select goals so narrow that they could be accomplished within a few weeks. Sometimes teachers set a goal only to realize, shortly into the school year, that the goal is not the most essential one given the needs of the particular group of students they are teaching. In such cases, we allow teachers to revise their goals and even applaud them for doing so. We have also experienced times when teachers face unanticipated obstacles in reaching their goals, and we have found ways to navigate through together, both principal-coach and teacher often learning tremendously in the process.

Guiding teachers to an appropriately challenging and ambitious goal takes some practice. The more comfortable you get leading with a coach's hat, the easier this process will become. As a principal-coach, you can make clear that the process is more important than the outcome—that the priority is setting a goal and working toward it with the overarching aim of helping students. Overemphasizing "results" can create a high-stakes culture that inadvertently encourages teachers to set a low bar that they know they can easily clear. If you are currently working to change such a culture in your building, please know that many teachers will need time and the experience of going through this process with you to realize that you are truly there to support and coach them, not to lay down a "heavy hand" if they don't reach their goal.

## Giving Feedback

Only after setting goals and observing teachers in their classrooms can principals embark upon the vital process of giving feedback. This process actually entails substantially more listening than speaking on the part of the principal-coach, whose goal is to empower teachers to take ownership of their professional learning. Hattie (2012) astutely points out that feedback messages to students are filtered through the students' perceptions, so what works as effective feedback for one student might not work with another. This insight applies to teachers, too, and underscores the importance of listening with sensitivity and striving to be as responsive as you can in adapting feedback to meet the needs of each teacher—including your most talented high achievers, who you might erroneously assume have the least need for feedback.

In *Fried: Why You Burn Out and How to Revive* (2011), Joan Borysenko writes that when high-achieving individuals—those who set challenging goals and work hard to achieve them—do not receive feedback, they are likely to experience stress, disappointment, or resentment, which can contribute to burnout. With all teachers, it is essential to remember that feedback is not a recipe that will result in success if followed with fidelity. Offering feedback requires a depth of human connection and understanding, along with openness, curiosity, and humility, as you and your teachers seek to improve the quality of learning in your school. In this section, we discuss some practical ways to incorporate feedback into your practice.

## Conversations

Although it would be ideal to follow up on every classroom visit with a conversation, we have found this to be virtually impossible for most busy principals and teachers. We thus schedule formal conversations with teachers throughout the year, typically three in addition to the post-conferences held for formal evaluation: one at the beginning of the year, one during the middle of the year, and one at the end of the year. During the first conversation, we set goals for the year. Midyear, we reflect on progress toward goals and make any course corrections that appear to be warranted. At the end of the year, we assess progress goals, celebrate successes, reflect on remaining challenges, and plan for next steps.

Among the tools we find helpful in these conversations is the ORID framework (Nelson, 2001) for coaches, which categorizes questions as *objective*, *reflective*, *interpretive*, or *decisional*. The ORID framework enables leaders not only to categorize questions but also to develop a logical sequence of questions that invite reflection and insight and point to next steps:

- **Objective questions** are easy to answer and are aimed at identifying pertinent facts and information, primarily in order to relieve stress and invite active participation. These are typically "what" questions, such as *What were the key points you noted about . . . ? What did you observe during the . . . ? What body language did you notice in the participants?*

- **Reflective questions** elicit emotional response and personal reactions, inviting a deeper level of participation. These questions ask, "What about 'the what'?" Examples include *What was the most/least successful thing you noted? What seemed to really work/not work? What concerns you/confuses you/annoys you? What was exciting, surprising, or frustrating about . . . ? How did you feel as you were . . . ?*

- **Interpretive questions** invite sharing and generate options and possibilities for the future, asking, "So what?" Examples include *What did you learn about yourself through this experience? What are things that you might have done/could do that would have enhanced/would enhance the outcome? What do these results mean to you in terms of future planning? What other ways could you assess . . . ? What insights have you gained about how you . . . ?*

- **Decisional questions** develop opinions, options, or solutions that lead to future actions, clarifying expectations for improvement or change. Essentially, these are "Now what?" questions, such as *What things will you do differently? What things will you do the same? Which of your skills will you further develop, and what will you do to develop them? What are your next steps? What supports will you need to continue to work on those areas?*

## Narrative Feedback

In addition to engaging in face-to-face conversations, we send written narrative feedback to teachers after every classroom visit, formulated in ways that are as low-effort as possible for principals but as high-impact as possible for teachers. An approach that we find effective and efficient is to offer nonjudgmental prompts connected to the teacher's goal, and then to remain open to teachers' reflections based on these prompts. Teachers are not required to reply to the principal but can if they choose to; the prompts are offered for teachers to use in whatever way makes the most sense to them. Such prompts include "I notice . . . " "I wonder . . . " "What if . . . ?" and "How might . . . ?" The following are two examples of feedback written in this style.

## Example 1

> Mr. Olson,
>
> When I visited your classroom today, I noticed that your class was transitioning with a brain break that let them practice compound words while singing and moving. The brain break appeared to have the effect of supporting students through a transition while simultaneously helping them practice their academics. Students also seemed to be having a remarkably good time. I wonder if you could start a Google Docs list to share with other teachers that they could add to as well?
>
> As you reviewed what students had previously learned (nouns, verbs), I noticed that you had students turn and talk. This seemed to give all students the chance to engage in thinking and responding. I did notice that they weren't always sure whom to talk to and often looked for their friends whom they weren't sitting by. I wonder if it would help to assign turn-and-talk partners or spend some additional time practicing how to quickly find a partner?

## Example 2

> *A compliment*: Students demonstrate engaged attention on close reading and are responsive to the guiding questions you pose. You offer an admirable mix of independent, paired, and full-class learning activities, thoughtfully integrated to meet student learning needs.

*Reflective feedback/questions*: I noticed the careful attention you were paying to the pacing of the lesson I observed, shifting from independent to full-class and then back to independent learning activities. I noticed scaffolded support in the form of written and oral questioning to guide students through a close reading of a story. I noticed you checking for understanding, discussing vocabulary they might not understand, and offering background knowledge to support comprehension.

I wonder what you notice as you observe the lesson concerning student comprehension. I wonder about the range of levels you observe in the classroom. I wonder about ways of assessing progress in learning.

What if students were even more aware of the specific comprehension skills they're working on? What if these skills were focused on in a range of disciplines?

How might we support students to self-assess their own understanding and their own progress?

Notice that the first example does not offer compliments or praise, which could undermine the nonjudgmental feedback, but does observe the positive effects of the brain break and the turn-and-talk activity. This is one way we have been able to achieve the tricky balance between showing appreciation and sharing nonjudgmental feedback.

In the second example, the nonjudgmental questions "What if?" and "How might?" are aimed at prompting reflective thinking as opposed to dictating what teachers "should" do. The compliment at the beginning represents another approach in our ongoing effort to demonstrate appreciation for the work teachers do while still offering nonjudgmental feedback.

In our narrative feedback, we strive to cite evidence of what we are observing rather than our own opinions. Here is an example:

> While students were working independently on their math assign-
> ment, you circulated the room to check on student progress, stop-
> ping to assist or give feedback to seven different students. When
> one student began to get off task, you used proximity and a touch
> on his shoulder to get him back to work without having to say
> anything.

If the practice of giving narrative feedback is new to you, then we suggest you spend some time practicing. The best way we've found to practice
is to watch videos of teachers in their classrooms and then write narrative
feedback for them. One of our favorite websites for watching great teaching practices is www.teachingchannel.org. After clicking the "Videos" tab,
you can filter your search by grade level, subject, or topic. Because most
of the videos pause for the teacher to explain what he or she is doing, you
will not get the full effect of a classroom and may need to make some infer-
ences. Still, these videos provide a great opportunity to get into the groove
of writing narrative feedback.

## Using Digital Tools

We have found digital productivity tools to be a valuable support to
busy principals and teachers and encourage you to use any application
or tool you find helpful and to remain open to new possibilities as they
become available. We are fans of Evernote, a cloud-based note-taking and
file storage application that synchronizes data across multiple devices,
takes photographs, and makes audio recordings. We and other principals
we know all have our own slightly different ways of using Evernote and
other digital tools.

For example, elementary school principal Matt Renwick, author of
*Digital Student Portfolios: A Whole School Approach to Connected Learn-
ing and Continuous Assessment* (2014), creates a digital notebook for each
teacher in Evernote. Teachers can view all of the feedback Renwick has
documented for them and also create their own notes in the notebook. As
Renwick visits classrooms, he can capture a variety of learning artifacts

within Evernote to share with the teachers, including images of students working, samples of student work, and audio recordings of students reading aloud or collaborating with peers. Renwick also writes notes to each teacher either by using the Penultimate app on his iPad, which syncs with Evernote, or by writing them on paper and scanning them into Evernote.

Prior to his more narrative approach to classroom feedback, Renwick had created a form that aligned with his school's focus on the gradual release of responsibility from teacher to student. On this observation form, Renwick noted where various components of the lesson fell on the gradual release of responsibility continuum: demonstration, shared demonstration, guided practice, or independent practice. (These four terms come from the work of Regie Routman and the Optimal Learning Model, an update on the gradual release of responsibility; visit www.regieroutman .org for more information.) These data were entered anonymously into a spreadsheet so that he could get an overall idea of where his school stood in terms of instructional practices. He looked at the data to help him answer questions like *Are we lecturing too much at the cost of giving students time to practice their skills in groups and independently?*

Unfortunately, Renwick discovered that his teachers, while appreciative of the narrative feedback, focused more on the tallies. He observed, "They would question the times I was coming in, or debate whether a part of instruction was demonstration or shared demonstration" (personal communication, December 17, 2016). Feeling this format to be unproductive for leading with a coach's mindset, he stripped away the tallying and focused exclusively on offering qualitative feedback. He retained the tenets of high-quality instruction, such as authenticity and engagement, to guide his commentary and help him discover trends and patterns in overall instruction.

The results? Teachers responded more positively to his classroom visits, both in their feedback to him and in their instruction. As Renwick noted, "We worried less about the numbers, which allowed us more time to talk about instruction as professionals" (personal communication,

December 17, 2016). This change in approach to instructional visits depended on the relationship between principal and teachers. Although technology did not get in the way, if it had been the function of Renwick's instructional walks, this improvement in leadership practice may not have occurred.

Another feature of Evernote is Skitch, a web-based tool that allows users to annotate pictures. With Skitch, a principal can use a tablet to take a photo of students during a classroom visit, write a comment on the photo and add an arrow to indicate what he or she is referring to, and then e-mail the note to the teacher.

## Complying with District Requirements

Your district may require you to complete an informal class visit form a certain number of times each year—for example, for four informal observations over a three-year evaluation cycle. As we established in Chapter 2, principal-coaches will not be satisfied with the minimum requirement and will offer continuous nonjudgmental feedback to teachers. It is also important to take some time to reflect on the purpose of your district's form, asking yourself, *Does this form provide my teachers with feedback to help them reflect on their practice, or does it just give them a checklist of things I saw?* If it's the latter, you have two options: (1) bring this concern to your district administrative team or the appropriate "higher-up" to see about making a change, or (2) use the form, but provide your teachers with additional narrative feedback, written or verbal, to help them become more reflective practitioners.

When using a district-required protocol for classroom visits, avoid a bean-counter mentality. Although checklists can provide a useful common language and set of expectations for classroom visits, they can be frustrating for administrators and teachers alike and may need to be supplemented with narrative observational data. It is important to remain cognizant that the overall purpose of classroom visits is teacher development, not teacher measurement.

# Dealing with Ineffective Practices

"If you permit it, you promote it" is an adage referring to the all-too-common practice of allowing ineffective or inappropriate practices to go unaddressed—for example, when a teacher notices but fails to confront a colleague who is wasting instructional time or disrespecting students. Principals are also guilty of such avoidant behavior. We do sympathize to some extent: confrontation is tough. But knowing that such practices are occurring and not addressing them allows a toxic environment to fester. If the principal won't address such issues, then who will?

Principal-coaches may see a conundrum here: if their goal is to lead with a coach's hat, how can they address ineffective practices without damaging the relationships and rapport they rely on to coach their teachers? We're sorry to report that there is no magic solution to this predicament. Although we believe that we have good relationships with the majority of our teachers and have engaged in numerous productive coaching conversations, we know that we are sometimes seen as the "bad guy" when we address ineffective practices.

Unless a teacher is doing something that is harmful to students or completely neglecting their duties, we try to address situations wearing a coach's hat rather than an evaluator's hat. For example, one principal we know made a morning visit to a 2nd grade classroom to find that the teacher was unaccountably screening *Finding Nemo* for her students, making no obvious connection to learning. The principal met with the teacher later that day and simply asked, "I visited your classroom today and noticed that you were watching a movie; can you tell me about that choice? The purpose wasn't clear to me." The teacher explained that the kids had been getting "squirrelly" from being inside at recess every day owing to the extreme cold and just needed to do something fun and laugh. The principal then brainstormed with the teacher alternative activities that would address the students' state without wasting instructional time. Although the principal could just have addressed the situation by delivering a written or verbal directive not to show movies, that would have been seen as disciplinary by the teacher as well as her colleagues. Instead, the principal was able to coach the teacher and help her come up with other options so that the next time the students got "squirrelly," she would be able to give them a brain break or use movement activities tied to their learning.

Shifting from judgmental to nonjudgmental feedback can be challenging. In all honesty, there are times when we walk into a classroom and feel the upset and judgment rising within us. At those times, we must reflect on whether we truly need to address what we are observing with an evaluator's hat or whether we can reframe our immediate reactions as nonjudgmental feedback. Figure 4.1 shows a chart we have compiled that offers possible ways to remain in a nonjudgmental coaching stance in the face of less-than-stellar teaching.

Figure 4.1

## Reframing Negative Reactions as Nonjudgmental Feedback

| What you would like to say . . . | What you can say with a coaching mindset . . . |
| --- | --- |
| "Please tell me you did not plan for this lesson. You winged it, right?" | "I wonder what your primary considerations were as you planned this lesson. I wonder what additional considerations you think might be helpful as you plan your lessons moving forward." |
| "You are so negative when you talk to students." | "I wonder what emotions students may have experienced as you spoke about your disappointment in the quality of their work. How might you support them to achieve the high goals you have set for them?" |
| "It's time to get off of your butt and circulate the room." | "I noticed that six students were solving the math problems incorrectly during independent practice time. How might you recognize and address misconceptions before students engage in extensive independent practice?" |
| "I am never going to get that 30 minutes back, am I?" | "What were your goals for this lesson? Which of them do you believe you accomplished? What are other possible ways to accomplish these goals? What might your next steps be?" |

| What you would like to say . . . | What you can say with a coaching mindset . . . |
|---|---|
| "It was obvious you just put on a dog and pony show." | "How did your use of the think-pair-share strategy enhance student learning and engagement during this lesson? How did it build on previous learning experiences students have had in your classroom? What did you notice about student ability? How might you use your observations to design learning experiences moving forward?" |
| "Do you even like kids?" | "Is everything OK? I've noticed lately that you've been quite short with your students and just wanted to see if there's anything going on that I can support you with."<br><br>*Whether this teacher always treats students this way or is just having some off-days, asking a question out of genuine concern opens the door for the teacher to share his or her struggle. This is an opportunity to show your support while letting teachers know that they should not take out what is going on in their lives on their students.* |
| "You wasted so much time in that lesson that your class will be a year behind the others." | "I wonder what the learning goals are for this lesson and how they connect to the learning goals for the unit. I wonder how you are prioritizing the many learning goals that are incorporated into this unit. How might you consider organizing time to prioritize learning goals for upcoming lessons?" |
| "Did you actually invite me in for a formal observation to watch your students read a play?" | "What feedback would be helpful for you to receive on this lesson?"<br><br>*This is a good reason why a principal should have a pre-conference with a teacher before coming in for a formal observation. If the lesson and objectives aren't conducive to an observation, the principal would have advance notice to reschedule.* |
| "Bueller? Bueller? Bueller? Bueller?" | "During your lesson, I noticed that you asked several questions that only a couple of your students responded to. You did give wait time and repeat each question, but no other students raised their hands. Why do you think the students who participated were the only ones raising their hands? Did you notice anything about the others that gave you any indication that they were engaged? What strategies might you use to engage students?" |
| "Where is your cooperating teacher?" | "I noticed that several students struggled with the concepts. Two of these students were special education students needing modifications. I also noticed that your co-teacher was not in the classroom during this lesson. How could he have offered support during this lesson? How might exploration into different models or purposes support you and your co-teacher in planning?" |

*Continued*

Figure 4.1 *continued*

# Reframing Negative Reactions as Nonjudgmental Feedback

| What you would like to say . . . | What you can say with a coaching mindset . . . |
|---|---|
| "Zzzzzzzzzz. . . . Oh, um, er . . . you're done already?" | "I noticed over the course of the lesson that almost all students asked to go to the bathroom or get a drink or engaged in activities not related to the lesson. I wonder why students appeared so distracted. How might you structure lessons to help students remain engaged?" |
| "The SMART Board is *not* meant to just project from your overhead!" | "I wonder how integrated educational technology has enhanced the quality of the learning experiences you provide. How might additional professional learning help you extend the potential of educational technology to support student learning in your class?" |
| "So when you describe your lesson planning as, 'I open the teacher manual and just start instructing,' you are actually *reading* the manual, correct?" | "What are your goals for this lesson? What are the resources you have used in addition to the teacher manual? How might you seek out additional resources to enhance teaching and learning?" |
| "When you are ready to start teaching, just wave." | "I noticed that 10 minutes elapsed between the time students entered your room and the time you began the lesson. I noticed that when you then sought to engage students, it took an additional 3 minutes to direct them to take out their books and pencils. How might you implement routines in a way that could help students transition and be ready to learn more quickly?" |
| "On a scale of 1 to 10, with 10 being the highest, how much do you like the sound of your own voice?" | "I wonder what the ratio is of the amount of time you were speaking to the amount of time students were speaking. I wonder how you might extend the duration of student speaking time. How might you design learning activities to encourage greater levels of student participation?" |
| "Leave. Right now. Don't come back." | *There's no coaching feedback for this kind of reaction. If you have already identified areas needing improvement and offered support and specific suggestions for improvement, and the teacher is so ineffective that you think he or she should be dismissed, then you need to get going on the necessary documentation to do so.* |

# Conclusion

When you provide feedback to teachers, it's important to recognize that you cannot and should not expect to be an expert on every aspect of instruction. Rather, your role is to provide teachers with objective evidence of what you observed and to follow up with open-ended questions that foster reflection. Wearing a coach's hat necessitates more listening than speaking as you empower teachers to take ownership of their own professional learning.

As you move toward providing teachers with nonjudgmental feedback, there may be times when you have a critical initial reaction and need to step back. When stepping back doesn't help and you find you can't resolve a challenging situation wearing a coach's hat, don't put off the difficult conversation you know you need to initiate as an evaluator. If you have a serious concern about a teacher's instruction, then your main fear should not be the conversation with the teacher, but what happens to students if you *don't* have that conversation.

## Put On Your Coach's Hat

*Reflect on your current reality:*

- Have you been giving teachers true feedback, advice, praise, evaluation, or none at all? What changes would you like to make to improve the quality of your feedback? If you are already giving feedback as a coach, how might you strengthen your practices?

- Reflecting on your feedback to teachers, do you provide a positive-to-negative ratio of at least 3:1? How are you nurturing your teachers?

- When you go through the formal observation process, are you more focused on the paperwork side of the evaluation or on the conversation with your teachers? Do you think they would perceive the process the same way? Do you complete the written evaluation before you meet with a teacher, or do you leave room to make additions after the discussion?

- How is goal setting a part of your teachers' practice?

*Continued*

- Based on your reflections above, set a goal to help you better provide feedback with a coach's mindset. Use the example goals on pages 91–92 to determine goal, action steps, supports, and evidence of progress toward the goal. Take this a step further and share it with your supervisor or trusted colleagues, or show your commitment to ongoing learning by sharing it with your staff.

- Practice writing narrative feedback to a teacher using nonjudgmental prompts like "I noticed . . ." "I wonder . . ." and "How might . . . ?" If your teachers are not used to receiving such feedback on an informal basis, then we suggest leaving off the "How might . . . ?" component until they are comfortable with coaching feedback. If you do not have teachers in the building right now, then go to www.teachingchannel.org to watch teaching videos and practice writing out your feedback or imagine having a conversation with that teacher.

- Decide what method of writing up feedback for teachers will work best for you, since you will not have time to meet with them after every visit. Consider such options as Evernote, Google Docs or Google Forms, e-mail, or just handwritten notes. Use whichever method will be most efficient for you. If you are going to create a notebook or folder for each staff member, then take the time to set up your system now. If your teachers have already written their professional goals for the year, then include each teacher's goal at the top of his or her notebook or folder so that you can see the goal before entering the teacher's classroom and provide feedback that applies to that goal.

---------- Five ----------

# Time: Managing Your Most Precious Resource

*There is never enough time to do everything, but there is always enough time to do the most important thing.*

—Brian Tracy

As a first-year principal in a new building, Melanie had every intention of providing the type of learning leadership that faculty members said they had been craving from their previous principal. She had plans to get into classrooms each week for informal observations and to meet with teachers regularly to reflect on student progress and provide feedback.

Yet once she was on the job, Melanie was continuously bombarded with pressing issues: students being sent to the office for discipline, parent complaints demanding immediate attention, and other urgent matters, including a paraprofessional quitting without notice and a shortage of substitute teachers. How could she ever find the time to get into classrooms when she was being inundated by a flood of issues that seemed to be conspiring to keep her in the office? She began to see why the previous principal hadn't been a learning leader.

Can you relate to Melanie? Have you experienced the same struggle in your position as a school leader? We understand all too well how busy, demanding, and complicated school administrators' day-to-day jobs are, and we know how impossible the goal of getting into classrooms can feel, with all of the unexpected events that occur on any given day. Kim Marshall (2003) has coined the term "hyperactive superficial principal syndrome" to define this ongoing cycle, referring to the immense time and effort a principal can put forth each day without ever stepping foot into a classroom.

Despite all the tasks and emergencies that keep us drowning in work, we have found that the more time we spend in classrooms, the better we can build rapport with students and converse with teachers—and the fewer fires we need to put out. One of the most common reasons principals give for not being able to visit classrooms is dealing with student discipline. This is also one of the biggest reasons why you *should* be in classrooms. You probably already know before the school year begins which teachers are going to have the most student discipline problems and which teachers are going to elicit the most parent complaints. (*Tip:* If you are a brand-new principal to your school, just ask the secretary.) Usually, the teachers with the most student discipline issues have failed to establish a supportive classroom community with consistent routines, procedures, and expectations. We would bet that the teachers most targeted by angry parent phone calls have similar discipline issues and may also be assigning too much homework.

What about your rock-star teachers? Before we began consistently leading with a coach's hat, too often we overlooked our finest teachers. If students and parents were happy, then so were we, ready to leave well enough alone and focus on trouble spots. We were not drawn into those classrooms of excellence. The result of this benevolent negligence was that our rock-star teachers lacked the collegial interaction they needed to move from great to even greater. Their natural aspirations for improvement stagnated, and their excellent ideas weren't disseminated throughout the school community. Knowing what we do now, we should have encouraged other teachers to observe these star practitioners, set up peer coaching models, and otherwise spread the wealth of the great teaching occurring in our schools. Elite athletes would not consider functioning without a coach, so why should exceptional teachers have to go it alone?

All this is to say, the better you're able to observe what's happening in classrooms and pinpoint areas of concern and excellence, the better you can help *all* teachers improve, and the fewer fires you are going to need to put out. Instead of being a "firefighter" who constantly reacts to issues as they arise, you can become a proactive "fire preventer" who nips problems in the bud by helping teachers build their capacity to effectively teach and manage their classrooms.

As our own leadership roles have evolved, we have learned that time management is just as important a skill as coaching. You can learn everything you want to about instructional coaching and having critical conversations with teachers, but if you can't figure out how to get out of your office, you will never be able to use your insight and expertise to foster improvement in your school. Although our priorities as learning leaders have shifted to spending more time cultivating our teachers' growth, the myriad duties and demands of our principalship remain. To lead as a principal-coach and help your teachers become top-notch practitioners, the key is working smarter, not harder. This chapter will help you hone your time management skills so that you are able to focus on your core mission of high-impact learning leadership.

## Managing Your Time

In Chapter 3, we explored the importance of relationships and trust. One way leaders unintentionally break trust with teachers is by overcommitting and being unrealistic about what they can accomplish. Think of how many times you have promised to follow up on something in a meeting or conversation—saying you will purchase additional teacher resource books on a particular topic, make a change in the schedule, set up an additional meeting, or contact a parent, for example—and then let it fall through the cracks. Unless you have built a task into your daily workflow of adding impromptu commitments to your calendar or to-do list, it is very easy to say, "I'll do that," and then completely forget to do it.

This issue is exacerbated by teachers' reluctance to "hound" their principal. Instead of asking where you are with said commitment, they remain silent and grow resentful about the fact that you haven't done it. Each time you agree to do something and fail to accomplish it, teachers' trust breaks down a little more.

So what is an overworked school leader to do? It is essential that you have a reliable system to help you schedule your day's meetings, classroom visits, and work tasks. In addition, you must recognize the amount of time you have and be realistic about allotting it. When you agree to do something, be honest about when you will likely accomplish the task. It is much more respectful to say, "I will not be able to get to that this week, but I can certainly do it next week," than to promise, "Sure, I'll do that," and then leave people hanging for weeks.

Although it would be ideal for all principals to have an assistant principal to help with the endless managerial paperwork and tasks that come their way, that's not the reality for many. Fortunately, over the years, we have learned and implemented a variety of workflow methods that make it possible to keep up with all the "stuff" while spending time coaching teachers.

With today's ever-changing technology, the menu of tools that can help with time management is boundless. The web-based tools we recommend in this chapter are, of course, not the only tools available; new ones seem to be created every day. We use tablets or mini-laptops to keep up with work out of the office, and we have found that a Wi-Fi–capable handheld device makes our work lives much easier to manage. If you do not have a small laptop or handheld device, we highly recommend that you invest in one. These devices enable principals to manage their time and workload much more efficiently, and there are very reasonably priced options. That said, in the following sections we offer alternative suggestions when possible for those who don't have access to such tools.

# Tips for Effective Scheduling

*The key is not to prioritize what's on your schedule, but to schedule your priorities.*

—Stephen Covey

The adage "What gets scheduled, gets done" may not be true all of the time, but it does speak to our priorities as leaders. One of the most important things we have learned over the years is to live by a calendar at school. A calendar can help you figure out your priorities and ensure you spend your time on work that matters and that will pay off in the long run. We make it our goal to spend as much time as possible observing in classrooms and meeting with teachers for reflective dialogue. This happens because we schedule it in our calendars. This section will help you set up and maximize the utility of your calendar.

## Setting Up and Monitoring Your Calendar

What does effective scheduling look like? A visual we find helpful draws from Stephen Covey's (1989) story about a man trying to fit rocks, gravel, and sand into a jar. The only way he could fit all three was to put in the big rocks first, then put in the gravel, and finally pour in the sand to fill the spaces in between.

The lesson here is that if the big rocks don't go in first, they won't fit at all. We tend to give more attention to the urgent and minor matters in our day (the gravel and sand) without prioritizing the "big rocks," like visiting classrooms and engaging in reflective dialogue with teachers. Thus, our first step in creating our calendars is to determine the nonnegotiables that must be included before other, lesser duties. To be an effective learning leader, you've got to prioritize coaching as one of the biggest rocks.

Begin as early as you can—ideally, in August—by filling in all you can in your own professional calendar to be ready for the school year. (No matter when you are reading this, do it now!) There will be regular meetings that you are required to attend; fill those in. Then determine the percentage of your time that you would like to dedicate to learning leadership in the trenches: spending time in classrooms, observing, modeling, and offering feedback. Then put that time in the schedule, in whatever way makes sense for you. Some leaders like to schedule two hours daily, whereas others prefer to schedule larger chunks of time, like a day and a half each week. Reflect on your own schedule and determine what would work best for you.

We also advise getting individual teacher meetings on the schedule far in advance, before the school year starts. Looking at your list of teachers, simply spread out the meetings across your calendar so that you meet with each teacher roughly every quarter. Depending on how large your school's staff is, you could plan to meet more or less frequently. The meetings provide opportunities to engage in reflective conversation about professional goals, share how the teaching and learning year is progressing, celebrate accomplishments and growth, and plan how teachers can use supports within and outside the school to foster their own learning and growth as professionals. These meetings are also great opportunities to build the rapport and relationships that are essential to effective coaching.

At the beginning of the year, distribute this schedule and share your goal of making regular classroom visits. Explain to teachers that these meetings are their opportunity to bring up anything they would like to discuss, including feedback they have for you, and ask that they come to the initial meeting prepared to answer one question: "What is one thing I [the principal] could change that would make a difference for you in your work here?"

Once you've entered your big rocks and required meetings, keep adding to the calendar and tweaking as needed throughout the year; you can

even color-code it (e.g., coloring classroom time red to signal its importance). As your year gets going, it is important to make regular check-ins
with your calendar and your priorities. Set aside 5 minutes at the end of
each day and 15 minutes at the end of each week to review your progress.
Is your calendar aligned with your priorities? What's getting in your way?
How can you plan accordingly? How are you coming along with classroom
observations (both formal and informal)? Are you following your schedule of meeting with teachers? Have you been in classrooms enough to be
able to engage in reflective dialogue during the following week's scheduled teacher meetings?

Taking this time to check in and monitor your progress ensures that
you are putting the big rocks in your jar first. You may even find that if you
increase this reflective time to 10 minutes daily and 20 minutes weekly,
you will have time to deeply reflect on your practice through journaling.

## Rethinking the Open Door Policy

Many school leaders pride themselves on their open door policy, seeing
it as an emblem of their school's culture of trust and rapport. Implementing the policy tells all members of a school community that the principal
wants them to feel free to come to the office at any time, and the principal
will stop what he or she is doing to listen to whatever they have to say. In
theory, the open door policy sounds great: what principal wouldn't want
to be the type of leader to whom staff members feel comfortable going
with any concern, at any time? In practice, however, the policy falls short.
Think about it: if you follow the open door policy, your work and focus
are constantly being interrupted, and what is on your schedule becomes a
lesser priority than whoever comes to your door.

Here's what the open door policy looks like. You're sitting at your desk,
focusing on (and feeling stressed about) the budget report due to the district office by the end of the day. Actually, it was due yesterday, and you've
already received two reminder e-mails and a phone call from the superintendent's secretary. Then Mrs. Smith, one of your 6th grade teachers,

walks in and asks, "Do you have a minute?" "Of course," you say. You sit at the table with Mrs. Smith and listen to her tell you about the problem she is having with one of her students. You're not listening as intently as you should, because you just recalled a piece of the budget report that you forgot to include. Mrs. Smith is still talking, but now you're thinking about the meeting you have in 20 minutes and wondering how in the world you are going to get the report finished. Productivity guru David Allen says it best: "Much of the stress that people feel doesn't come from having too much to do. It comes from not finishing what they've started."

Having an open door policy makes it appear that you're open to hearing staff and parent concerns, but it paradoxically makes it harder for you to truly attend to those concerns as well as to manage your time effectively and proactively. When you schedule time in your calendar for meetings, classroom visits, and office work, you are able to mentally prepare for each part of your day and be fully in the moment, whether you are meeting with a teacher or working on that monstrous budget report.

### A Principal's Perspective

When Joan initially heard the case against the open door policy at a workshop for principals, she was not interested. She had always prided herself on the time she spent with her staff members, dropping everything to give them what they needed. However, she quickly came around when she realized that the policy was preventing her from making the best use of her time, and she returned to her building ready to devote more time to being in classrooms.

At her next staff meeting, Joan shared what she had learned. She admitted that she felt a bit uncomfortable making this change to her daily work but wanted to devote more time to being in teachers' classrooms and focusing on their individual needs, not distractedly thinking of whatever she had just interrupted to chat with her visitor. Joan had already talked with her secretary and decided that they would meet daily to discuss her calendar and have staff go to the secretary to schedule appointments with Joan. Joan acknowledged that just saying "schedule appointments" felt awkward, but she also recognized that the new system valued teachers' time as well as hers.

Does Joan now follow this new system 100 percent? No, but she tries to. If a teacher stops her in the hallway to tell her a story or ask a simple question, she walks and talks with the teacher. However, if a teacher has a concern that is going to require a lengthy conversation, she says, "Let's schedule a time to meet so we can discuss this," or "I'm going to a classroom for a formal observation; can we meet later today?"

The best alternative to an open door policy we have found is to enlist your secretary or office assistant to help manage your calendar and make your staff aware of this scheduling process. Using this system, you are more likely to stick to your schedule and be able to spend dedicated time in classrooms and in meetings with teachers while still accomplishing all of the other administrative work you are responsible for.

Giving the secretary access to your calendar ensures that he or she knows where you are throughout the day and is able to schedule appointments for you with any teachers or parents who request them. The secretary doesn't need to ask if you can meet with Mrs. Smith tomorrow, because he or she can already see on your calendar that you're free during Mrs. Smith's prep time.

Thanks to technology, this process has become much smoother than it used to be. We now carry a tablet with Wi-Fi access throughout the building to access our schedule on Google Calendar, which can be updated in real time by either the secretary or ourselves. Teachers who are comfortable using Google Calendar can even send you direct invitations to meet that you can accept, decline, or suggest a different time for. Many online tools can sync with Google Calendar, allowing teachers to schedule a meeting when you are available. There are many options to choose from, but we currently like using Calendly and ScheduleOnce. Figure 5.1 (see p. 116) shows a screenshot of a sample week scheduled in Google Calendar.

Figure 5.1

## A Screenshot of Google Calendar on a Tablet

Scheduled Meetings, Staff Calendar Events, To Do!, Culture Building    Sun Oct 23 – Sat Oct 29, 2016 (Central Time)

| | Sun 10/23 | Mon 10/24 | Tue 10/25 | Wed 10/26 | Thu 10/27 | Fri 10/28 | Sat 10/29 |
|---|---|---|---|---|---|---|---|
| 6am | | | | | | | |
| 7am | | Principal | Admin-Tech Mtg 7am - 7:20am | | Complete observation 6:45am - 7:30am | Maintenance 7am - 7:30am | |
| | | Professional Development Day 7:30am - 3pm | Pre-Observation: | IEP Mtg: SL 7:30am - 8am | IEP Mtg: AL 7:30am - 8am | Meet with RM 7:30am - 8am | |
| 8am | | | | Pupil Services 8am - 8:30am | Cover KM Class 8am - 9am | St Mtg: AM 8am - 8:30am | |
| | | | | Observation-JL 8:45am - 9:30am | | | |
| 9am | | | | | | | |
| 10am | | | Call Social 10:15am - 10:30am | Post Mtg: JL 9:45am - 10:05am | | IEP Mtg: GM 10am - 11am | |
| | | | New Student 10:45am - 11:15am | Observation: SM 10:30am - 11:15am | | | |
| 11am | | | | | | | |
| | | | Lunch/Recess Duty 11:30am - 12:30pm | Lunch/Recess Duty 11:30am - 12:30pm | Lunch/Recess Duty 11:30am - 12:30pm | Lunch/Recess Duty 11:30am - 12:30pm | |
| 12pm | | | Pre-observation: | Post Mtg: SM 12:30pm - 12: | | | |
| | | County Truancy Mtg 1pm - 3pm | Office work 1pm - 3pm | | Cover DB Class 1pm - 2pm | IEP: TW 1pm - 2pm | |
| 1pm | | | | | | | |
| 2pm | | | | | Call Math rep 2:15om - 2:45pm | | |
| | | | | | | Celebration 2:45pm - 3pm | |
| 3pm | | Admin Mtg -after truancy mtg 3pm - 4:30pm | IEP Mtg-TZ 3:15pm - 3:45pm | Detention duty 3pm - 3:30pm | | Admin Mtg 3:15pm - 5pm | |
| | | | | Data report for Board 3:30pm - 4:15pm | | | |
| 4pm | | | MAP Webinar 4pm - 4:45pm | | | | |
| 5pm | | | | | | | |

We call our alternative to the open door policy our "out and about policy." Implementing this policy means we are behind a door only when we absolutely need to be—for private conversations with teachers, parents, or students or when we need quiet, focused time to work on a task like a budget report or proposal. Saying "My door is always open" implies that we spend most of our time behind that open door, in our offices. Learning leadership requires our presence in the places where teachers teach and students learn and interact—primarily in classrooms, but also in our school libraries, gyms, cafeterias, hallways, fields, and playgrounds. So many of the most important learning conversations we have with teachers happen in their spaces, not in the formal setting of the principal's office.

## Scheduling Classroom Observations

Principals leading with a coach's hat get into classrooms both for scheduled formal observations and for frequent informal observations aimed at providing coaching feedback. Scheduling both formal and informal observations is important to help you stay focused on your coaching goals.

### Formal Observations

Each district's evaluation process dictates the number of formal observations you must conduct; the number varies from district to district. We advise looking at the number of teachers you need to formally observe and the number of observations required prior to the start of the school year and creating a reasonable schedule to share with teachers at the beginning of the year. This schedule is general, only identifying the teacher names for each month, but it lets teachers know when they should expect a formal observation and helps you stay on track throughout the school year.

At the end of each month, you or your secretary can send an e-mail reminder to the teachers who are scheduled for a formal observation the following month so that they can schedule a specific day and time with the secretary. When the secretary sets up an observation appointment, he or she also schedules the teacher for a 10-minute pre-conference and a 20-minute post-conference with you. The post-conference should take place the same day or the following day. We often find that the paperwork required for a formal observation can be difficult to complete within a day or two, but the conversation with the teacher is the most important part and should not wait for the paperwork to be ready for a signature.

### A Principal's Perspective

During her first years as an administrator, Jill spent a minimum of two hours on each teacher's formal observation write-up. She typed detailed descriptions for the indicators in each teaching standard, pulling from the detailed, scripted notes she took while observing in the classroom. Jill never seemed to have two hours to spare in a given day, so it often took her weeks to finish writing up an observation and schedule a time to meet with the teacher. By then, she found, the teacher usually only vaguely remembered the lesson that Jill had observed; often, the teacher was already immersed in the next unit of study, so any feedback Jill provided was too late and almost as irrelevant as state testing scores. During each post-observation discussion, she shared everything she had observed, including what was done well and what needed to improve. But because so much time had passed, it was difficult for the teacher to recall and reflect on the lesson. None of the information Jill provided led to reflection; the conference was simply a one-sided conversation focused on the "necessary paperwork" for a teacher evaluation.

When Jill changed her leadership perspective from an evaluative one to a coaching one, her approach to the post-observation process changed, too. Her priority now is to provide teachers with feedback that will open up a reflective dialogue. She no longer spends hours writing up a detailed report, fixating on it as something to be turned in to the district office for the teacher's personnel file; of course, that is still where it ultimately goes, but that's not the purpose she holds in her mind when she writes the report.

Now Jill schedules a time to meet with a teacher either the day of or the day after the lesson she observed so that they can reflect on the lesson while it's still fresh in their minds. For the conversation, Jill pulls up the notes she typed into her tablet during the lesson using her district's adopted observation form, but it is not a completed report. Instead, she uses her recorded observations to guide the discussion, offering feedback on what went well, bringing up an area that could be improved on, and asking for the teacher's thoughts on how that specific area could be improved. On a good day, Jill can complete the observation form after the discussion, but if it doesn't happen for a few days, it's OK: the teacher has already received immediate feedback and can start making any changes they discussed the next day. When Jill sends the completed report to the teacher to sign, it also serves as a reminder of what they discussed. In some cases, Jill's teachers add comments describing what they have already changed in their classrooms as a result of the post-observation discussion.

## Informal Observations

Our calendars fill up quickly with meetings, but we still make it a priority to schedule informal classroom observations. We schedule these visits two weeks in advance and make room in the calendar for two hours a day dedicated to classroom time. We do keep these appointments flexible as formal observations and other meetings are scheduled; if important meetings come up, we reschedule that classroom time to another part of the day, still keeping it a priority. The secretary can see the time designated in Google Calendar as "Classrooms." She won't know exactly where we are, but she knows to tell a parent or teacher looking for us, "I'm sorry, but the principal is in classrooms right now. Can I schedule a time for her to meet with you this afternoon?" A competent secretary is able to distinguish between a matter that requires the principal's immediate attention and an issue that can be put on the schedule.

### A Principal's Perspective

Jessica lives and breathes by Google Calendar. To ensure she gets into classrooms, she simply blocks off two hours each day as "Classrooms" on the calendar, varying the times as needed. Her secretary knows that if a teacher wants to schedule a formal observation or meeting during that time, he or she can; Jessica considers any meeting with a teacher part of that classroom time, because it provides an opportunity for reflective conversation and coaching. If she needs to schedule other types of meetings, such as with parents or a sales rep, then the block of classroom time is adjusted to another part of the day.

As proactive as Jessica is with scheduling informal observations, she does admit that it doesn't always happen. For example, as the district assessment coordinator, she spends a lot of time during state testing on tasks related to testing. There are also days when she finds herself swamped with student discipline issues that take up her time. If discipline incidents are not urgent—say, a bus referral for a student swearing on the afternoon route the previous day—she doesn't deal with them during scheduled classroom time but fits them in before or after other scheduled items on her calendar.

## Scheduling Office Time and Managing Paperwork

*Time is the scarcest resource and unless it is managed nothing else can be managed.*

—Peter Drucker

As we add classroom time and meetings to our calendars, we also schedule "office time" to complete those necessary tasks that have the potential either to consume all of our time or to be put off until they're overdue. Having been dedicated teachers who never sat at our desks when students were in the classroom, we do feel the "office guilt" of sitting at our desks when the building is full. Nevertheless, there are required tasks that we'd rather accomplish during the day than while our own families are at home having dinner without us.

To schedule this time, we use tools and apps that make it easier to keep track of what needs to be done while keeping our minds clear of all the details until it is time to work on the task. Some options include

- A free task management app like Remember the Milk, Todoist, or Toodledo.
- The Evernote reminders feature (if you already use Evernote for your organization system).
- A paid system like Omnifocus, which allows you to schedule and keep track of everything on your to-do list.
- Another calendar you create in Google Calendar, calling it "To Do" or "Tasks," in which you schedule each task you need to complete. The reminder feature of Google Calendar is almost as helpful as your secretary, prompting you when you need to work on something. If you live for crossing items off your to-do list, create an additional calendar called "Completed Tasks"; once you complete a task, you can edit the event to appear on your completed task calendar. This also helps you keep track over time of everything you do.

Your to-do list may include tasks like typing up two teacher evaluations, screening teacher candidate applications, or preparing for an upcoming faculty meeting. Whatever tasks you know you have to get done, putting them in your calendar helps you focus on them and execute them efficiently.

A note on sharing your calendar: we have learned that even though the secretary should be able to tell where you are by checking your calendar, it is best to be discreet when it comes to potentially sensitive details. If your secretary knows that you're working on an improvement plan for Ms. Evers, she may have a difficult time maintaining a poker face when they chat in the mailroom. We recommend keeping such details on your own task calendar, which the secretary does not have access to.

Now that you've put office time in the calendar, how do you keep track of all the paperwork? In the following sections, we discuss how to manage the deluge of paperwork (we consider e-mail "virtual" paperwork) you inevitably deal with as principal.

### The Tickler File

The tickler file is a simple organization system made prominent by "Getting Things Done" guru David Allen. More closely related to the education field, Justin Baeder (2010), director of the Principal Center, has helped principals learn about the power of this system to schedule paperwork for later without cluttering their desks now. Figure 5.2 provides a visual of the system.

Figure 5.2

## The Tickler File

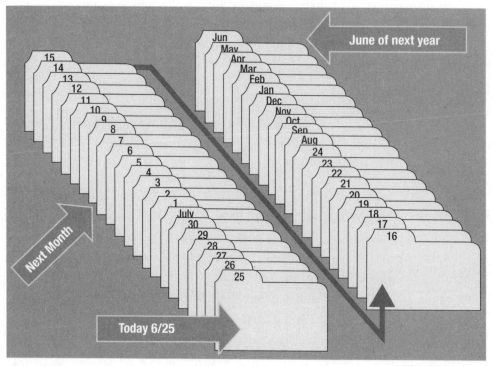

To set up your tickler file, you'll need 43 manila folders. Label 12 of the folders with the months of the year, and label the remaining folders with numbers 1–31. Place all of these folders in the file drawer that is closest to where you work at your desk. You will rotate the numbered file folders daily as you pull out each day's folder. For example, if today is March 24, you'll see the "24" folder in the front, containing all of your papers for the day, which could include paperwork or notes for meetings. Behind that folder will be folders 25–31, then the April folder, and then folders 1–23. After you take the papers out of folder 24, you will place that folder behind folder 23, in the April section. At the end of the day, you can put any unfinished paper items in the 25 folder or schedule them for another day and place them in the appropriate folder.

This system allows you to keep the clutter off your desk so that when you are working on an item, it is the only thing on your desk. This frees your mind from being distracted by the numerous other tasks yet to be completed, which are filed away for the day you are scheduled to work on them. We advise adding an item to your task calendar when you file something in a dated folder; this comes in handy if you need to find an item but can't remember when you were planning to work on it.

The key to this system's effectiveness is to use it daily. Some possible uses for the tickler file include filing flyers for future events, notes that you want to devote time to at a later date, or a reminder to check in on your progress toward a personal goal. The system is especially helpful for reminding yourself to follow up on things that you will likely forget. For example, if you are registering a team of teachers to attend a conference and know that you'll need to schedule it by October 10, you can file the registration paperwork in the October 7 folder to allow time for teachers to get back to you and for you to complete the registration.

You can also use the tickler file to manage bigger projects: the budget, a state report, the master schedule, or a professional development session, for example. In a Principal Center webinar titled "High Intensity Leadership," Justin Baeder (2010) shared a familiar predicament: our workdays just don't give us the big chunks of time we need to complete large-scale projects, so the projects often get pushed off for another day (and then another, and then another). If you find yourself in this situation, it may help to keep in mind that principals tend to work in 15-minute chunks due to the continuous interruptions that are a part of daily life in the school building. Rest assured that you have not developed an attention deficit; your mind has just gotten used to working in small chunks of time, and you have learned to be flexible with your time. Baeder advises principals to take advantage of this capacity by planning to complete big projects in 15-minute chunks.

Here's how it works. Write the title of your project (e.g., "Master Schedule for 2017–2018 School Year") at the top of an index card, and list the first step ("Create Excel spreadsheet with all time slots and teachers"). Take 15 minutes to complete that task, cross it off, write down the next step on the index card, and put it in your tickler file for tomorrow (or whichever day you plan to work on it again). Baeder points out that a project for which you have allotted four hours may actually take only eight 15-minute sessions to complete, because you will be completely focused on the task at hand during each 15-minute chunk.

## The E-Mail Beast

We would be remiss to discuss time management without addressing the e-mail beast. Some of us can remember the time when our main mode of communicating with staff was placing printed memos in their physical mailboxes. Although e-mail has certainly made correspondence easier, it can also be a major drain on our time.

Although handheld devices have made it easy to check e-mail from any location, this method of "keeping up" on the go may not be the most productive. Say you're scrolling through e-mails as you walk down the hallway, and you open up a message from a first-year teacher, Ms. Newby, and see that she forwarded you an e-mail from a parent who is outraged about something that happened in the classroom. Ms. Newby is asking to meet with you during her prep time at the end of the day. You know that as a novice teacher, Ms. Newby will need some guidance on how to handle this parent. While you're still reading the e-mail, your walkie-talkie goes off with a Code Blue alert, meaning you have to get to the special education classroom immediately to assist with a student who is being aggressive. By the time you've assisted the staff with a safe seclusion and restraint of the student, provided a follow-up debrief, and contacted parents, two hours have gone by. You try to salvage the remaining two hours of the day by visiting the classrooms you were scheduled to be in during this incident. The following day, you learn that Ms. Newby received a tongue lashing from the angry parent after school yesterday, and she is upset that she didn't have your support. She waited near your office during her prep time and feels that you ignored her.

This scenario isn't typical of how most "e-mail incidents" occur, but it makes our point: it is too easy to scan e-mails on the go, get distracted, and then forget to return to them. Just as your desk can pile up with paperwork that somehow needs to get done, your e-mail inbox can get very cluttered very fast. Once you have scanned e-mails, they're marked as "read" in your inbox, and you're not likely to notice them again and address them.

We suggest you treat your e-mail just like you did that pile of paperwork on your desk—get rid of it! Schedule time on your calendar for e-mail twice a day and aim for Inbox Zero. That's right: Inbox Zero. We promise that this goal is not a flying unicorn; it is actually possible to achieve, and on a regular basis. Here are tips to help you get there (or at least come close):

• Sit down for 10 or 15 minutes of scheduled e-mail time and crank through your messages.

• Don't touch an e-mail more than once.

• Don't use e-mail as your to-do list. Remember, you have a system in place now, so use it. If you read an e-mail that requires more than two minutes to act on, schedule when you're going to do it and move the e-mail from your inbox to an Action e-mail folder, or print it out and put it in your tickler file for the day you scheduled it.

• Don't let a read e-mail sit in your inbox. Schedule it and get it out of your inbox.

• Don't clutter up anyone else's inbox. Recognize when you need to go and talk instead of sending an e-mail.

• Take work e-mail off of your phone. No, you will not need a 12-step program to do this, and we promise you that the world won't come to an end. If it's on your phone, you are just scrolling through it, and you will not be able to accomplish the steps above.

## The Never-Ending To-Do List

> *This constant, unproductive preoccupation with all the things we have to do is the single largest consumer of time and energy.*
>
> —Kerry Gleeson (2009)

We all have it: the never-ending to-do list. We are convinced that even if time stopped to allow principals to catch up on everything, it would still be an impossible goal. We just have to learn how to meet deadlines while maintaining a system of workflow for everything else that comes our way, without having it pile up on our desks and prevent us from being in classrooms.

In his book *Getting Things Done* (2001), David Allen writes about setting up a workflow system that helps you have a "mind like water," a phrase used in karate to refer to the position of perfect readiness. Allen observes that when you throw a pebble into a still pond, the pond responds "totally appropriately to the force and mass of the input; then it returns to calm" (pp. 10–11). His message with this metaphor is to avoid overreacting or underreacting. When you have a mind like water, you are able to focus appropriately on the task at hand, complete it or decide when to return to it, and move on.

We all know what it is like to have our minds running, constantly thinking of tasks we haven't finished or items we forgot to add to the calendar.

By having a system where you can store all of these random thoughts, you keep your mind free to focus on what's happening in the moment. The specific system you use is up to you. Some principals like to cover their desk and computer monitor with sticky notes, but that often leads to a cluttered landscape of notes that makes it hard to maintain focus. Others maintain one running list, rewriting it each day or week. This system can work, but if it contains short-term, high-priority items alongside tasks due a month from now, you may have a difficult time focusing on what you need to do today.

The key to success with any system is to review it daily and as often as you need to in order to get all the extraneous "stuff" off your mind so you can focus. This may mean opening up your task management app once an hour; all it takes is 15 seconds to see if you're on track for the day, decide whether to move an item to the following day, and return to what you were doing. This is why it is so handy to have a handheld device that allows you to check your to-do list no matter where you are.

### A Principal's Perspective

Melanie was drowning in sticky notes and tired of recopying her to-do list every day. She needed to see what was essential to accomplish each day while being able to add ideas that popped into her head while sitting in a classroom so that she could quickly write it down and then get back to observing student learning.

So Melanie scrapped the sticky notes and created a simple Word document that she printed out each week and fastened to the clipboard she carried throughout the building. The document was filled with tables labeled "phone calls to make/e-mails to write," "meeting/newsletter ideas," "items for my office assistant," and so on. Now that Melanie has a tablet, she uses the Remember the Milk app to maintain her to-do list, but her system remains essentially the same: when she is out and about, anytime she thinks of something that she needs to do, she simply adds it to the pertinent list. She checks the app frequently to see what she needs to work on when she returns to her office. Figure 5.3 shows what her system looks like.

Figure 5.3

# To-Do List

| Items for staff meeting agenda | Items for next newsletter | Support staff items |
|---|---|---|
|  |  |  |
|  |  |  |
|  |  |  |

| E-mails/phone calls to make | Weekly staff update items | Office assistant |
|---|---|---|
|  |  |  |
|  |  |  |
|  |  |  |

| To do | Evaluations/teacher support | Admin items |
|---|---|---|
|  |  |  |
|  |  |  |
|  |  |  |

Notes:

## The Paperwork Side of Classroom Visits

In our early days as principals, when we used class visit checklists, we checked off boxes on carbon-copied paper and left a copy on the teacher's desk before leaving the room. It was an efficient system, but it didn't provide teachers with opportunities to reflect on their practice.

As we kept learning and developing our practice, we tried to have individual conversations with teachers after each visit. We soon learned that that was not feasible if we planned to be in classrooms frequently. So we developed simple forms with lines to write on, printed on colored paper, or purchased large sticky-note pads on which to leave written feedback. This worked, but having been trained to "document, document, document," we needed to photocopy each note before giving it to the teacher and then file our copy, as well as use a spreadsheet on a clipboard to keep track of which teachers we visited and which we still needed to visit and when. All of these steps added up to a somewhat inefficient process.

Our classroom observation systems were continually evolving; as we made tweaks and changes, we kept considering the question *What is my purpose?* Was it simply to check off a box on a spreadsheet confirming that we were in that classroom on a given date? Did we need to note whether we provided written or verbal feedback? What if we had multiple copies of a simple two-column spreadsheet with teacher names on the left and a larger column on the right? We could use this to write any notes about that observation. This spreadsheet also told us when we had visited every classroom and needed to start a new spreadsheet, ensuring that we didn't visit some classrooms more than others. Principals who don't keep track of which classrooms they visit may not realize that they tend to pay more visits to the classrooms closest to the office or to those with the strongest teachers.

When tablets and mini-laptops came on the scene, things got more streamlined. We found it easier to stay out of our offices for longer periods, because we were able to access our e-mail and many other handy tools remotely. In addition, these new devices took the hassle out of providing written feedback, since there was no need to provide handwritten notes, make copies, and then file the notes.

We found ways to meet our district requirements while going beyond the minimal requirements for "informal walkthroughs" and "formal observations" and using web-based tools on our handheld devices to keep track of our classroom visit progress and feedback to teachers. It is an individualized system that continues to evolve, but the following vignette provides a snapshot of how such a system looks in action.

After the morning announcements, elementary school principal Rob checks in with his secretary and then has enough time to sign a stack of timesheets and other district forms. At 8:15, it's time to follow his calendar and devote the next two hours to visiting classrooms. Rob opens the Evernote app on his tablet to the note that includes the current checklist of teachers in his building. Evernote enables users to create checkboxes, which makes it easy for him to keep track of which classrooms he has been in and which he hasn't.

When Rob has visited every classroom in turn, he pulls up the master list of teachers and copies and pastes it into a new classroom visit note, entering a new date at the top. Each of his classroom visit checklists in Evernote lists the dates from when he began that set of walkthroughs through when he completed them. Rob tries to get to each classroom every two weeks. Sometimes he manages to get through all of them in a week; during busy periods, such as test prep time, it can take up to three weeks. Rob admires principals who say they visit each classroom daily, but he knows he can't do that if he wants to provide teachers with feedback while keeping up with everything else on his plate.

Today, after Rob looks at the names of the six remaining teachers on his list, he pulls up his district evaluation tool to see that he still needs to complete the first documented walkthrough for two of these teachers. He opens the required forms and uses them during the walkthroughs for each of these teachers, documenting teaching and learning behaviors he observes while in their classrooms. For example, he noted for one teacher,

> The teacher asked several questions requiring students to respond in multiple ways, such as using think-pair-share and written responses and calling on volunteers and nonvolunteers. By using this variety of responses, the teacher held all students accountable for thinking and responding. The teacher circulated the room to check students' written responses, answering a few student questions and providing support to a struggling English language learner.

When Rob submits the district-required form, the software program will automatically e-mail a copy of the form to the teacher. He checks each of the two teachers off his Evernote list and then opens the Simple Goals app on his tablet and taps on his "Classroom Visits" goal so it can keep a running tally of how many classroom visits he's made. The running tally for the day, week, and month provided by this simple tool keeps him motivated.

When Rob visits other classrooms, he observes for about 10 minutes and then, depending on what the class is doing, may walk around to see student work, ask individual students what they're learning, or even jump in to offer support or feedback to students. He is actively involved with a lot of students, knowing many of them from leading intervention groups and the 1:1 check-in/check-out program for students struggling with behavior issues. Teachers have expressed their appreciation for his jumping in to help as well as offering any insights he has on individual students. Either before or just after leaving each room, Rob opens up Evernote for that teacher's individual note—he has a note for each teacher that he can easily find by the "tags" feature—and begins to compose a note containing simple narrative feedback on his main observation while in the classroom. An example follows:

Ms. Boston,

When I visited your classroom today, I noticed that you were modeling writing for your students. You modeled writing two sentences, spelling words kindergartners would probably spell using Jolly Phonics and referring back to the Jolly Phonics sheet they have in their bins. You also modeled how to draw a picture that matches your writing, emphasizing the importance of the picture matching the story so it makes sense. You had lots of kiddos excited to choose "Work on Writing" after this! I sat and watched a few students doing Work on Writing and noticed them applying everything you had modeled. I noticed that Brandon was able to go right back to a page he had previously written and make a picture to go with it. I wonder how many of your kindergartners are able to go back to their journals and independently find what they had worked on on a previous day without your assistance?

Once Rob is satisfied with his draft, he copies and pastes it into an e-mail and sends it to the teacher. Rob has now e-mailed feedback to the teacher while keeping documentation for himself. He often receives e-mailed or verbal replies from teachers as they reflect on his feedback. Rob has heard of other principals using a Google Form to record narrative feedback. With an added script, the Google Form automatically e-mails the teacher the feedback that was entered. This would be another easy method to use if Rob had not already been happily using Evernote.

For a while, Rob was curious about how well he was following through on giving feedback to teachers, so he created a Google Form to help him keep track. The form was simple, just requiring him to select the teacher and his method of feedback (none, handwritten, district form, e-mailed, verbal—conversation, or verbal—quick) for each classroom visit. The results were eye-opening: Rob was shocked by his lack of follow-through with some teachers, and he was surprised to see that the feedback he did provide tended to follow certain patterns for specific teachers (e.g., Mr. Ramirez always received "verbal—quick" feedback, while Mrs. Cooper got e-mailed feedback). This exercise gave him plenty to reflect on. Although tracking his feedback this way is not required or even his main focus, Rob continues to take this additional step as he completes his classroom visits and reflect on his feedback statistics each month.

## Finding Balance When Demands Are High

Many dedicated principals operate with a "people during the day, paperwork at night" mentality. We spend most of our school days in classrooms, with teachers, and with students. We spend long, late evenings with paperwork and clock countless hours in the office over the weekends, sometimes even bringing our own children into a classroom to play while we work in a corner of the room. Maybe you can relate to being sleep-deprived, over-caffeinated, and often cranky with your own family members, who can feel like they're low on your list of priorities. You may even be working at a rate that you fear you cannot sustain in the long term. If this is the case, then you have even more reason to refine your time management and organization skills and revise your "people during the day, paperwork at night" approach. By honoring your time, you will also be a better leader during the day, especially if you are feeling balanced on a personal level.

When educators take on the principal's position, they know that they will be carrying a heavy load and working long hours. However, the job does not need to be life-consuming. Near the beginning of this chapter, we asserted that no matter how much you know about instructional coaching and critical conversations, if you can't figure out how to get out of your office, you will never apply your knowledge to foster improvement in your school. We also feel strongly that if you do not take time for you and your family to achieve balance in your life, it will be difficult to sustain your role as a leader for your staff, your students, and your community. Just as you use your calendar to schedule priorities at school, you can use it to schedule personal or family activities to make them a priority.

# Conclusion

In *The ONE Thing: The Surprisingly Simple Truth Behind Extraordinary Results* (Keller & Papasan, 2013), Jay Papasan notes that the most important thing he has learned from his experiences is that "the most successful people are the most productive people . . . productive people get more done, achieve better results. . . . They do so because they devote maximum time to being productive on their top priority, their ONE Thing." We believe that the ONE Thing that can make an incredible impact in our schools is to be in classrooms and converse with teachers wearing our coach's hat—and we need to protect our time with a vengeance to be able to do so.

Principals are exceptionally busy. They wear many hats, have many demands placed upon them, and must deal with constant interruption throughout their days. To lead a school to greatness, the principal must serve as a learning leader, dedicating a great deal of time to being in classrooms and conversing with teachers while wearing their coach's hat. To achieve this, principals must become efficient at managing their time and all of the other "stuff" on their to-do lists. Throughout this chapter, we shared ways for you to become more efficient by

- Setting classroom and teacher dialogue time as priorities, or "big rocks," in your calendar, even scheduling observations and individual meetings before the start of the year.

- Managing your schedule with the assistance of your secretary and a digital calendar and changing an open door policy to an "out and about policy" to help you dedicate your attention appropriately.

- Providing teachers with feedback on classroom management to help curb student discipline issues that are better dealt with by teachers.

- Scheduling office time for the necessary tasks you must complete.

- Organizing your paperwork in a tickler file to keep your desk and mind free of distracting clutter.

- Protecting yourself from future burnout by not letting your job consume all of your personal and family time.

If you believe you have a lot of room to grow in time management and organization, then understand that just reading this chapter will not make you perfect at it, or even solidly efficient, tomorrow. Take on one section of this chapter each week, and build the new habits into your daily routine until you feel you have it down. Only then should you add something new. Come back to this chapter at the end of each week to reflect on how your time and task management went, and pick a new strategy to implement the following week.

## Put On Your Coach's Hat

*Reflect on your current reality:*
- What "fires" are you called on to put out on a regular basis? Are they getting in the way of your being in classrooms?
- What needs to change in your current day-to-day reality to enable you to be in classrooms? Make a list, including things that seem impossible (e.g., no students get sent to the office, the time-consuming PTO president gets a job and stays out of the office, the secretary becomes more efficient and is able to take on more of the tedious work that she should be doing).
- How efficient are you at the paperwork side of your job? Are you doing it late at night instead of spending time with your family? Can you find what you need in your office and get tasks done on time? Are you able to keep track of what's due and when before the district office calls to tell you you're late, again?

*Next steps:*
- Begin each day by identifying your three "big rocks" for the day. Add time in your calendar at the end of the day to reflect on your big rocks. Did you accomplish them, or did you let sand and gravel take over? What are your three big rocks for tomorrow?

*Continued*

- Spend some time right now on your schedule. If you don't currently have a solid calendar system in place, then decide what you're going to use, whether it be paper, Google Calendar, or another online system that your secretary will have access to. If you're in the middle of the school year, work on your schedule for the next two weeks to calendar in classroom time as well as the to-do tasks you need to complete.

- Schedule a meeting right now to meet with your secretary to explain how you will be sharing your calendar. Explain that in order to be an effective learning leader, you need to spend more time in classrooms and that he or she can help you do this by managing your calendar when people come looking for you. Teach your secretary how to add events to your calendar. Make sure to check in each day for the first couple of weeks to see how it's going.

- If you don't currently have an organized system for paper-work and a clean desk that allows you to work without distraction, then set up a tickler file—better yet, ask your secretary to create the folders for you. Then sort through the piles on (and maybe under) your desk, putting to-do items into the appropriate folders and scheduling them on your calendar. You may find that you have papers that just need to go in the shredder.

- Decide which tool or app you want to use for your never-ending to-do list: a "Tasks" or "To Do" calendar in Google Calendar (making sure to use the reminders feature), Remember the Milk, Todoist, Toodledo, or Omnifocus. Feel free to research other options that work better for you.

# Six

# Transforming Your School into a Team

We opened this book with a question: *If schools were teams, what would the role of principal be?* The sad reality is, many (if not most) schools are decidedly *not* teams. Only 7 percent of U.S. teachers say that their school has a strong collaborative model, and more than 50 percent claim never to have seen a colleague teach (Barkley, 2016). Take a moment and consider that statistic: more than 50 percent of U.S. teachers, despite spending every day in schools full of other teachers, have *never* seen another teacher in their school actually teach.

In some schools, the reality is even more distressing, with active infighting among teachers. Faculty rooms become spaces of bitter lament. Policies, initiatives, working conditions, salaries, administrators, and even other teachers are the sources of upset and the targets of complaint.

Usually, lurking just below the anger, gossip, and mean-spiritedness are vulnerability and pain. Teachers who entered the profession filled with idealism and optimism, seeking to make a positive difference in the lives of students, find themselves feeling unappreciated, professionally isolated, and overwhelmed by the enormity of expectations and student needs.

The best way to counteract alienation and burnout and create a positive, collegial school culture is to transform your school into a team. As Pasi Sahlberg (2015), former director general at the Finnish Ministry of Education, points out, "The quality of an education system can exceed the quality of its teachers if teaching is seen as a team sport, not as an individual race" (para. 29). He adds that "teachers need greater collective professional autonomy and more support to work with one another. In other words, more freedom from bureaucracy, but less from one another" (paras. 30–31).

Transforming teaching from an individual race into a team sport is arguably the single most important goal for principal-coaches. Yet even school leaders who are extraordinarily skilled in coaching teachers often struggle with this goal. Thus, in this chapter, we turn our attention from individual coaching to helping faculty coalesce as a team.

### Teachers' Perspective

Geri and Susan have taught 4th grade in adjacent classrooms for the past 14 years. With different teaching styles and a wide range of interests, they have much to share with each other and truly enjoy their weekly grade-level collaborative planning time. Because Geri and Susan trust each other so much, they were surprised by the anxiety they both felt when their school's newly hired instructional coach suggested that they observe each other teach. Despite their apprehension, they were intrigued and agreed to explore a range of ways to approach classroom visits. Some of their coach's suggestions felt awkward, even overwhelming, while other ideas she offered had more appeal. Through these conversations about classroom visits, Geri and Susan recognized how professionally isolated they had been without even realizing it. Their new instructional coach prompted them to wonder, *Might there be another way?*

## Instituting Teacher-Led Classroom Visits

"Get out of your office and into classrooms" has been one of our most consistent messages to aspiring principal-coaches. That advice is essential, yet ultimately insufficient. An equally important call to action is "Get your teachers out of their own classrooms and into the classrooms of their colleagues." When principal-coaches empower teachers to use instructional coaching techniques to support one another, they inspire their school to evolve from a collection of independent practitioners into a high-functioning, cohesive team. This shift, arguably more than any other, has the potential to transform schools.

Inviting teachers to enter their colleagues' classrooms sounds simple enough; after all, classroom doors are unlocked and often wide open during teaching time. On the surface, there seems to be little preventing teachers from visiting one another. Yet those who spend their days in schools recognize that the reality is far more complex and that many teachers will resist the idea of collegial classroom visits.

Teachers' initial concerns typically relate to logistics: *Will the school schedule allow for classroom visits? How much time will classroom visits require me to spend out of my classroom? Who will take over teaching my class while I am in another class? Will I need to give up planning time? If so, will I be paid for my time?* Each school's situation is different, but working around these challenges requires creativity. Savvy educational leaders will think through logistical issues (scheduling, budget, coverage) ahead of time and prepare as many solutions as possible.

The next level of concern often relates to workload: *How much time will class visits and follow-up conversations take? Even if my class is covered by a substitute when I visit another class, how much will my students miss by my not being there, and how can I make that up? Will planning time be taken from me? If so, how will I complete everything I need to accomplish?*

Proactive planning to manage teacher workload and shift schoolwide priorities is vital to enable teachers to dedicate the time needed to participate in classroom visits.

After concerns about logistics and workload are addressed, deeper hesitations often surface. Some teachers are concerned that having other adults in their classroom will weaken their professional autonomy. Others suspect that the feedback they receive will be contradictory, vague, or impractical. Numerous teachers do not trust administrators' ability to structure peer classroom visits in ways that are helpful to student learning. Many have never experienced professional collaboration involving visits to other classrooms and cannot yet imagine the benefits. Perhaps the most poignant concern is anxiety, stemming from raw vulnerability. At ease among their students, many teachers feel profoundly uncomfortable at the prospect of inviting others to observe them as they teach.

We teach from the core of who we are as individuals, transmitting far more than content and skills. When we teach, we reveal ourselves. There is a bravery that is rarely celebrated or even acknowledged in the depth of self that teachers bring to their students. Inviting other adults into these interactions, especially other skilled adults who will be able to offer sound critique, can be intimidating.

Kindness and respect are the antidotes to these deeper concerns, along with a genuine commitment to supporting one another to become better versions of ourselves. Nurturing a culture of openness and nonjudgmental consideration of areas to improve is perhaps the most important task for principal-coaches who are striving to transform their school into a high-functioning team. As we delve into a range of pragmatic, flexible approaches to opening classrooms to colleagues, we remain cognizant of the vulnerability inherent in the process and the need for sensitivity, humility, and understanding.

## Approaches to Designing Classroom Visits

Teachers' opening up their classes for colleagues to observe is a coura-geous act, as their shortcomings, insecurities, and questions are revealed along with their strengths and successes. As principals visit classrooms and structure faculty classroom visits, they should have tremendous sen-sitivity to the vulnerability of teachers who open themselves, whether by choice or requirement, to other professionals.

Principals who encourage teacher-led classroom visits are also acting with courage, empowering teachers to take control of their professional learning while remaining accountable for the results. For principals who have embraced the recommendations of this book and become more pres-ent and engaged in the teaching and learning happening in their schools, the shift can be at once exciting and disorienting. As teachers' classroom visits flourish, principal-coaches will no longer be directly involved in some of the most important professional learning occurring in the school. Feeling a mix of emotions—pride and excitement as well as a sense of loss and exclusion—is natural. As teachers discover ways to engage meaning-fully in one another's classrooms and collegially explore, question, and strive, embracing the values and approaches the principal has champi-oned, the principal will be able to evolve as well, nurturing the strengths of the school as a whole rather than merely those of individual teachers.

There are so many reasons to postpone class visits; so many other pri-orities that require principals' and teachers' attention. Sensitive to the range of difficulties involved, we have identified four basic approaches to teacher classroom visits that help teachers get acclimated to and comfort-able with the process. These include (1) visiting other schools, (2) begin-ning with a small number of interested teachers, (3) beginning with one grade-level team or department, and (4) schoolwide implementation with preparation.

Transforming a collection of teachers who essentially function as independent contractors into a team will look different in every school. Among principal-coaches' most significant tasks is to nurture this process, assessing the readiness of individual teachers and the school as a whole and making choices about how to progress. The following approaches can be adapted or mixed and matched to meet the unique needs of each school.

## Approach 1: Visiting Other Schools

A good way to ease into teacher classroom visits, particularly in a school with a culture of teacher isolation, is to organize visits to other schools and provide time for follow-up reflection. Going to another school has two primary advantages for schools embarking on teacher classroom visits for the first time: (1) it's an easier, gentler way to begin because it doesn't require teachers to immediately open themselves up to colleagues, and (2) the logistics for arranging visits to other schools are typically simpler for schools that have not yet adapted their schedules and structures to accommodate regular faculty classroom visits.

A significant disadvantage to visiting other schools is that, like one-shot workshops, a single outside visit is highly unlikely to result in substantial (or even minimal) improvement in teaching and learning. It best serves as a kick-start to collaboration and connection and an opportunity for teachers to gain insight on the value of learning from and with colleagues, not merely in workshops or seminars but by being together in the classroom and then reflecting on the experience. In follow-up conversations, principals can identify which teachers seem most open to making classroom visits within the school.

Coordinating visits to other schools involves a range of logistical considerations for administrators. One approach is to schedule as many teachers as possible to visit different schools on a professional development day. Although this is in many ways an ideal approach, as teachers are already scheduled to engage in professional learning and there are no classes to cover, it can be challenging for schools with larger staffs to find a sufficient number of schools to accommodate all teachers on one day. In such cases, principals can determine how many teachers it is possible to send to other schools on a particular professional development day and plan alternative professional learning experiences for the rest. In some schools, it might make sense to schedule visits throughout the year, sending small groups of teachers on different days and covering their classrooms with substitutes. An advantage to this approach is that it will be easier to find schools to accommodate visits from everyone over time; a disadvantage is the expense and challenge of providing substitute coverage for the teachers who are out. Some schools may simply decide to limit the number of teachers who visit other schools to make the coordination more manageable and gradually open the opportunity to additional teachers as feasible over the course of several years.

To maximize the value of an outside school visit, we advise scheduling time for teachers to engage in reflection together both prior to and after the visit. Entering another teacher's classroom, whether in one's own school or in someone else's school, demands respect and kindness. We suggest discussing in advance the importance of expressing gratitude to the host teachers and discussing the visit in follow-up conversations in appreciative and nonjudgmental terms. We also recommend that teachers plan in advance any questions they have and think of the areas they are most interested in, so that they gain experience focusing a classroom observation on a particular question or problem of practice. The follow-up discussion will be more powerful if it invites teachers to reflect not merely on what they observed but also on how what they observed relates to their own teaching and on what questions it raises for them about themselves as teachers and as learners.

Visits to other schools aren't just for schools beginning the practice of teacher classroom visits; this traditionally introductory, low-impact approach to class visits can be adapted as an advanced, high-impact approach for schools or even districts with mature, collaborative cultures of professional learning that are ready for deeper exploration. As part of the Kansas City Great Schools initiative, for example, almost 200 educators visited a wide range of schools nationally and internationally to learn about the approaches of high-performing public schools serving similar populations to that of Kansas City. And the traditional Singapore American School (SAS) sent professionals on visits to more than 100 schools in seven countries. According to SAS superintendent Chip Kimball, "It transformed our thinking and created a sense of urgency for change" (quoted in Vander Ark, 2016, para. 16).

## Approach 2: Beginning with a Small Number of Interested Teachers

A more direct yet still manageable approach to beginning classroom visits in schools new to the practice is to start with a small number of interested teachers who volunteer to participate. As these teachers learn together, stretch their thinking, and improve their craft, creative synergy thrives and momentum grows as more teachers choose to get involved in classroom visits. Although not all teachers will voluntarily participate, no matter how inspiring the principal-coach is, there is a tipping point when there emerges a sense of the school as being more than a collection of individual professionals. At that point, the school is on its way to becoming a team.

## Approach 3: Beginning with One Grade-Level Team or Department

A variation on working with a small number of teachers is engaging the members of one grade-level team or department (or a few teams or departments) in visiting one another's classrooms. This approach enables the principal-coach to work with a "micro-team" that models how the school as a whole might function as a team. It also promotes the development of leadership skills among faculty team leaders and department chairs. As the teams involved meet with success and teachers speak positively about the class visits, more teams and departments will participate, enhancing collaboration and collegiality simultaneously within teams and departments and throughout the school as a whole. In time, the practice can be extended to engage teachers in visiting classrooms outside their own team or department.

### Approach 4: Schoolwide Implementation with Preparation

Sometimes it makes sense to just *go for it* and introduce schoolwide class visits for all. This is best accomplished in schools that have already established a positive culture of trust and whose teachers have embraced classroom visits from school leaders. Going this route requires tremendous preparation: anticipating and addressing logistical issues, creating schedules, and coordinating coverage for teachers who will be missing teaching time to participate. You'll need to provide a comprehensive explanation of the reasons for the practice and what it entails. Make sure to provide faculty with the opportunity to ask questions and offer input: showing respect for the perspectives and contributions of all provides an inspiring model of how you want your school to function. Going this route is certainly ambitious, but it's a strong approach if your school is ready for it, and there's a palpable excitement when everybody is launching the new practice together.

## Structuring Classroom Visits

There is no proven recipe for structuring classroom visits, no formula that can guarantee success. There are, however, a range of options that can be adapted to meet teachers' and schools' specific needs. These include peer coaching, in which teachers use techniques of instructional coaches to support one another; instructional rounds or learning walks, in which groups of teachers visit classrooms, reflect together on what they have observed, and design a plan of action based on their findings; and lesson study, in which teachers create a lesson together, observe as one of them teaches the lesson, and then reflect on the lesson with the goal of improving their craft. All of these structures ask participants to

1.  Determine a *problem or question of practice* related to teaching and learning that is directly observable, is actionable, connects to a broader strategy of improvement, and has the potential to have a significant effect on student learning.

2.  Observe and gather evidence related to the problem or question of practice through such activities as examining student work samples, conducting interviews with students and with teachers, creating lesson plans, visiting classrooms, and analyzing video recordings of classrooms.

3.  Reflect on the evidence gathered and determine action steps accordingly.

In the following sections, we explore peer coaching, instructional rounds, and lesson study and look at how each structure incorporates these three foundational steps.

No matter which structure you choose for your school, teacher classroom visits will likely challenge prevailing norms of teacher privacy and result in some skepticism and awkwardness, or even fear and anger. Teachers will be asked to engage in unfamiliar behaviors, in some ways paralleling those adopted by principals who take a coach's approach to leadership. They will be invited to observe and to be observed, to notice details of what they are observing without judgment, to reflect and to support their colleagues to reflect, and to stretch their own thinking as they imagine potential action steps based on their discoveries. The discomfort that results from these new practices is disquieting yet ultimately necessary and healthy. As Elizabeth City and colleagues noted in *Instructional Rounds in Education,* "If the process did not result in awkwardness and disequilibrium, it would not effect any significant cultural transformation" (City, Elmore, Fiarman, & Teitel, 2009, p. 11).

Each of the three structures discussed here is nonjudgmental and has no connection to formal evaluation (City et al., 2009; Stephens, 2011). The choice of which structure or combination of structures to adopt depends on a wide range of factors, including faculty readiness, school culture, available resources, logistical considerations, and the specific goals your school wants to achieve. Once you have selected a structure, you can adapt it to meet your school's unique needs in a variety of ways.

## Peer Coaching

Peer coaching is, in its simplest terms, one teacher helping another to improve. The different forms peer coaching can take are limitless and as unique as the teachers who participate in them. Teachers participating in peer coaching may plan together, analyze colleagues' instructional practices and provide feedback, expand or refine their skills collaboratively, demonstrate effective teaching through modeling or team teaching, explore ways of implementing new strategies with colleagues, or observe colleagues' lessons and reflect on what they saw. It is a nonevaluative process focused on supporting teachers' professional learning (Foltos, 2013; Robbins, 2015). Because peer coaching at its essence requires little more than two interested teachers and can take as little or as much time as teachers choose to invest, it is a wise choice for principal-coaches who face substantial teacher skepticism about classroom visits.

If your school has a particularly strong culture of isolation, you can begin the process gently, with collaborative work that does not initially include classroom observations. Collaborative work engages two or more professional colleagues in informal interactions that focus on topics of mutual interest and do not push teachers to substantially stretch their practice or even their thinking. As trust and confidence build, along with support in the school for peer coaching, faculty members can graduate to a process of formal peer coaching in which they engage in a pre-conference, a classroom observation of a lesson, and a post-conference focused on teaching practices that enhance student learning.

Coaching can occur between two experienced teachers, an experienced teacher and a less experienced teacher, or an expert and a novice. One teacher serves as the inviting teacher, who will be observed, and the other as the coach. Except in the case of peer coaching between an expert and a novice, the participating teachers reverse roles so that each has the opportunity to be observed and to observe.

Here's how the three basic steps introduced on page 146 are incorporated in the peer coaching process:

1. The teacher who will be observed (the inviting teacher) identifies a problem or question of practice during a pre-conference.

2. During a classroom observation of a lesson, the observing teacher gathers evidence related to the problem or question of practice.

3. The teachers reflect on the evidence gathered and determine action steps during a post-conference.

During the pre-conference, the inviting teacher explains the question or problem of practice he or she has selected—typically something the teacher is genuinely curious about, which might have an instructional, a curricular, or a student emphasis—and describes the lesson to be observed. Together, the two teachers determine what data will be collected and how it will be gathered. Throughout this process, the inviting teacher is respected as a researcher in his or her own classroom, and the coach serves as the data collector. During the pre-conference, the coach supports the teacher in planning the lesson, typically by asking probing and clarifying questions to help the teacher articulate the problem or question of practice he or she is exploring and fine-tune the lesson. At the end of the conference, the coach asks for feedback from the teacher on the quality of the conversation, allowing the coach to reflect on which coaching strategies are helpful and which might need to be refined. In the early stages of a peer coaching relationship, it is typical for the inviting teacher to choose a problem or question of practice that is likely to yield positive data. As trust builds between partners, and they have the opportunity to switch roles and observe each other, they become more comfortable experimenting and taking risks.

During the post-conference, the coach shares the data collected and asks questions that prompt the inviting teacher to reflect on his or her practice with regard to the question or problem being investigated. Many observing teachers report that the most difficult part of the coaching process is deciding what questions to ask and how to word them. This step is challenging and requires practice. At the end of the post-conference, the inviting teacher gives feedback to the coach, enabling the coach to further reflect on and refine his or her coaching skills. During the next peer coaching cycle, the pair reverses roles. A positive, collaborative relationship between peer coaches is vital. It is important for teachers to be able to choose their partners and to stop working together if the relationship is not functioning well (Robbins, 2015).

### A Principal's Perspective

Janet, a veteran principal, had not herself learned about brain-based teaching. However, several teachers in her building had read everything they could to continue their learning on this topic. Janet witnessed firsthand how the strategies they put in place helped them increase student engagement and improve classroom management. She added these strategies to her mental "tool bag" of strategies she consulted during coaching conversations with teachers who struggle with student engagement and classroom management. She was completely honest in sharing that she learned these strategies from other teachers in the building, and offered to cover classes for teachers to go and observe brain-based strategies in action. Janet learns from the teachers in her building each day, and by spending her time in classrooms is able to share knowledge to help all teachers achieve their personal best.

### A Principal's Experience with Peer Coaching: Amy's Story

Amy, recently promoted to principal of the middle school where she has spent her entire career, has tremendous admiration for the skill and dedication of the teachers with whom she works. As an English teacher and then as the English department chair, Amy enjoyed

*Continued*

professional camaraderie and close friendships with the other teachers in her department. Her school has always scheduled weekly department meeting time, and Amy appreciated engaging in rich collegial conversations about curriculum, programs, and students.

When Amy was promoted to assistant principal a few years ago, her school was embarking on a serious exploration into ways of making the teacher supervision process more powerful. Amy's principal decided that it would be important for Amy to spend substantial time in classrooms and in follow-up conversation with teachers. Finding the classroom visits and reflective conversation to be profoundly meaningful, Amy devoured books on instructional coaching and connected with other school leaders committed to integrating these approaches into their supervisory process. Before long, Amy fully embraced leadership with a coach's hat.

Because Amy spoke so effusively about the benefits of classroom visits, a number of teachers expressed tentative curiosity about the practice. Wanting to lead by example, and still teaching one class herself, Amy opened her own classroom to any colleagues who wanted to observe. Balancing humility and masterful teaching, Amy invited colleagues' observations and used their feedback to support her ongoing efforts to improve her own teaching.

Amy's biggest regret was that she did not have the time to explore teaching and learning as deeply as she would have liked to with each of the 60 teachers she supervised. It occurred to her that just as she sought to empower her students to direct their own learning, she could empower teachers to direct their own professional learning. She imagined the potential of a network of educators, visiting one another's classrooms and reflecting together on high-quality teaching and learning. When she was promoted to the role of principal, implementing peer coaching became Amy's top priority.

Amy initially reached out to teachers who had observed her teach and invited them to partner with a colleague to visit each other's classrooms. A number of teachers jumped at the opportunity and served as the school's vanguard, experimenting with formats of peer coaching. Although they read some books on peer coaching, mostly they created their own approaches, adapting as they discovered what worked well for them and what they might refine. Once a cadre of teachers had gained comfort with their own home-grown approaches to peer coaching, Amy invited them to share their experiences in department meetings throughout the school. In time, more and more teachers participated in peer coaching, which gradually transformed the culture of the school into one of far greater collegial engagement and investment.

Amy's experience demonstrates ways principal-coaches can, with patience, engage in the process of transforming schools into teams. Peer coaching was an early step in the process that led to a range of other practices. We'll return to Amy's story after delving into a description of the next structure she adopted: instructional rounds.

## Instructional Rounds

A variety of approaches to classroom visits inspired by the practice of medical rounds have flourished, referred to as instructional rounds, teacher rounds, or learning walks. For our purposes, we will simply refer to *rounds*, emphasizing the similarities in each of these approaches and, as relevant, pointing out alternative approaches to implementation.

Principal-coaches who are ready to move from coaching individual teachers to nurturing a team often choose to implement rounds. Teachers engaging in the approach function as a network, using coaching techniques collaboratively to improve not only individual practice but also the practice of the school as a whole. Just as principal-coaches share nonjudgmental feedback to support teacher reflection, educators participating in rounds collect nonjudgmental evidence, not connected to formal evaluation, to prompt collaborative reflection on teaching and learning and identify areas of need that can inform professional development. Rounds are descriptive and analytical, helping educators understand what is happening in classrooms, consider how the school as a system produces the effects observed in classrooms, and reflect on what the school or district can do to address the identified problem or question of practice (City, 2011).

Rounds are an inquiry-based process, sometimes implemented by schools and sometimes by entire districts, sometimes engaged in exclusively by teachers and sometimes by building or district administrators as well. Here's how the three basic steps introduced on page 146 are incorporated in this structure:

1. A problem or question of practice is determined either by teachers or by the principal, depending on the approach being implemented, that connects either to teacher interest or to the school improvement strategy. As a variation, a grade-level team or department can use rounds to identify and explore its own problem or question of practice (City, 2011; Troen & Boles, 2014).

2. A network of educators is convened—typically, 8–30 teachers who are then divided into smaller groups of 4—and observes and gathers evidence related to the chosen problem or question of practice. Each group typically visits four classrooms and stays for 20–25 minutes in each. Observers don't have rubrics because they are gathering descriptive data rather than assessing against a rubric; instead, they usually have focus questions related to the problem of practice. They also question students about what they are working on, what they do when they don't understand something, and how they know whether their work is good or great.

3. The network convenes to debrief, reflecting on the evidence gathered, identifying next steps, and building the group's relevant knowledge and skills. Different networks experiment with different ways of formulating the next level of work. Some brainstorm action steps to be completed in the next week, in the next month, and by the end of the year. Others generate reflective questions to prompt further thinking. The process of rounds is repeated regularly (City, 2011).

The primary purpose of rounds is generally not to give feedback to those being observed but, rather, to help the observers reflect and learn about themselves. Although rounds do have an effect on individual practice, the method is designed to improve the school as a whole. That said, many educators find that it feels disrespectful not to offer some feedback, and adapt the method to offer nonjudgmental feedback to those they observe.

Rounds can be far more naturally implemented in schools where teachers are used to being observed by and engaging in reflection with a principal-coach. Rounds can also be a logical next step in schools that have already engaged in some form of peer coaching, where teachers feel comfortable being present in one another's classrooms. As schools prepare to embark on rounds, they should consider a range of possible approaches, determine what makes most sense for their needs, and then adapt the method used over time based on feedback from participating educators. For example, in a variation of the rounds approach referred to as *teacher rounds*, a host teacher teaches an individual lesson while others in the rounds network observe. The teachers then meet and offer feedback to the host teacher. Each teacher in the network ultimately has the opportunity to serve as host teacher. Although this model, like other rounds structures, emphasizes classroom observations and follow-up conversation within a network, it differs in that only one classroom is visited per rounds cycle rather than four or more classrooms, and the observation is followed with a formal session offering nonjudgmental feedback directly to the teacher observed (Troen & Boles, 2014).

The guiding principle of a rounds group is that all adults are committed to the success of all other adults. Participating teachers make a collective commitment to some course of action and are accountable to one another, rather than to a formal authority, to fulfill the agreements they make (City, 2011; City et al., 2009). Thus, rounds offer principal-coaches a powerful way to help teachers move from an increasingly archaic 19th century model of personal accountability to a 21st century model of collective responsibility. In making this shift, three norms are relevant:

1. Teachers need to be open to expressing conflicting views about teaching, embracing the productive disequilibrium that may arise.

2. Teachers need to become increasingly familiar and comfortable with ambiguity.

3. Teachers must collectively commit to continue their work together amid ambiguity and conflict.

### A Principal's Experience with Instructional Rounds: Amy's Story

Let's revisit Amy several years after her promotion to principal. Peer coaching is now flourishing at her school, engaging many teachers in collegial classroom visits and follow-up reflection. Amy herself has made great progress in leading with a coach's hat: she now consistently sets professional goals with each teacher, visits classrooms regularly, shares reflective observations with teachers after each visit, and meets with each teacher three times a year for more in-depth conversation. Benefiting from the long-standing practice in her school of weekly scheduled department meetings, Amy has dedicated professional learning time to assisting department chairs and teachers to use department meetings more effectively, focusing on teaching and learning rather than on programming and administrative logistics. She now feels ready to take the next steps toward transforming her faculty from a group of individual professionals into a high-functioning team.

Through her own work with a leadership coach and with other principals dedicated to leading with a coach's hat, Amy has learned about the practice of instructional rounds. Her coach, a former principal himself, is convinced that her faculty is ready for rounds and that the practice has the potential to propel them forward as professionals.

Amy begins by informally talking to teachers who have had positive peer coaching experiences. When Jonathan, the math department chair, expresses interest in instructional rounds, she invites him to lead the new process for the entire faculty. Looking at the budget and schedule, Amy finds that she will be able to reduce Jonathan's teaching load to give him time to dedicate to facilitating instructional rounds.

Jonathan prepares by reading extensively about instructional rounds and learning walks and by speaking with administrators and teachers in other schools who have adopted various versions of the approach. In conversation with Amy and a group of interested teachers, Jonathan designs an approach that he believes will work for their school. They plan to schedule instructional rounds once a week for the entire academic year and to include 15 teachers in rounds each week. Each group of 15 teachers will constitute a network and will work closely together throughout the year. With 60 teachers in the school, each network will be able to participate in rounds once a month. This level of frequency is essential to Jonathan and Amy, who are committed to embedding rounds in the professional life of the school not as an "event" but, rather, as a routine closely connected to the rest of the professional learning and collaboration occurring within the school.

Faculty members, many of whom already feel comfortable visiting one another's classrooms, overall respond with enthusiasm when Jonathan and Amy present their plans for instructional rounds during professional development in August. Jonathan and Amy have prepared extensively by anticipating logistical concerns, assigning teachers to rounds groups, scheduling rounds, and providing for coverage of any classes that teachers will miss during rounds. They appoint a facilitator for each of the four rounds networks and have each network meet to choose its problem or question of practice.

One network decides to look at ways educational technology is used in classrooms to support learning; another chooses to explore the degree of choice and independence students experience in

*Continued*

classrooms; the third plans to examine how teachers incorporate formative assessment into classroom learning experiences; and the fourth decides to look at classroom design and how classrooms' physical setup and aesthetics facilitate learning. Because the networks are heterogeneous, composed of teachers from different departments and grade levels, it makes sense for them to explore broad topics that are relevant to all teachers in the school.

Jonathan facilitates one of the rounds networks himself and meets weekly with Amy and the other three rounds facilitators to discuss implementation of rounds, sharing successes and brainstorming ways of overcoming challenges. Amy and each of the other members of her educational leadership team participate as equals with faculty members in instructional rounds.

Each week, members of the participating rounds network check in to review the problem or question of practice they're exploring, conduct 10-minute visits to six classrooms, and reflect afterward on what they noticed, what they wonder about, what they imagine about their own teaching based on the visits, and what next steps they might recommend for the school (typically collaborative or professional learning opportunities for teachers). At the end of the academic year, each network presents its experiences and gleanings about teaching and learning to the rest of the school. They then critique the experience together, sharing what went well, how they would like to refine the rounds practice to be more effective, and recommendations for professional learning the following year. The network facilitators then meet with Amy, refine the practice of instructional rounds for the following year, and make decisions about schoolwide next steps for professional learning based on their classroom observations and reflections.

Through the experience of instructional rounds, the four facilitators grow as a team, as does each of the four networks. The facilitators wonder about ways of extending teacher collaboration even further. When Jonathan attends a math conference and learns about the Japanese practice of lesson study—typically, although not always, used to develop math learning experiences for students—he is intrigued. He brings the notion back to Amy, who is enthusiastic. Jonathan also shares what he has learned about lesson study with his own math department and finds that his colleagues, now comfortable visiting classrooms and being observed by other teachers, are ready to try it.

The influence of instructional rounds in Amy's school was far-reaching. Teachers began to think more deeply about teaching and learning, to view one another with increasing respect, and to experience a sense of commitment not only to their students but also to their school as a whole. They began to experience themselves as a team.

Amy's evolving experience demonstrates how principal-coaches can get other school leaders and faculty members invested in the process of becoming a team. Whereas peer coaching served as a vital step in this transformation, instructional rounds prompted Amy to empower Jonathan and several other colleagues to lead as facilitators and to invite all teachers to visit one another's classrooms and reflect together on teaching and learning. As a key leader in the process, Jonathan gained the confidence to set even more ambitious goals for faculty collaboration, setting the stage for the school's next quantum leap forward. We'll return to Amy's and Jonathan's story after delving into an explanation of the lesson study approach.

## Lesson Study

Often viewed as the "gold standard" for enhancing teacher knowledge, lesson study is an advanced method of professional learning appropriate for schools already functioning as highly effective collaborative teams. Developed in Japan, lesson study is a powerful structure that has teachers plan lessons together, observe these lessons being taught in actual classrooms, and discuss their observations. Generally, although not always, participants in a lesson study group teach in the same grade-level team or department. This may not be feasible in smaller schools, so teachers can also work together to create lessons even if they will not all be teaching the same lesson.

A lesson study cycle begins when a group convenes to create a detailed lesson plan, drawing on past experiences, observations of their current students, and a range of curricular resources. Sometimes, teachers look to the school's mission statement and the qualities it espouses, such as curiosity and inquisitiveness, and consider ways of nurturing these qualities within their students rather than focusing exclusively on specific academic skills.

After creating the lesson plan, teachers observe as one member of the lesson study group teaches the lesson to his or her students. Afterward, the group meets to reflect on the lesson, sharing observations and offering suggestions. After this discussion, some groups will begin a new cycle with a new lesson, whereas others will choose to revise and reteach the lesson so that they can continue to learn from it. If a group chooses to revise the lesson, a second member will teach the new version to his or her students while colleagues observe. The teachers then reconvene to share their observations, comments, and suggestions for this revised lesson.

Here's how the three basic steps introduced on page 146 are incorporated in lesson study:

1.  The lesson study group determines a problem or question of practice, which often relates to qualities of character included in the school's mission statement.

2.  The group observes and gathers evidence from a range of different sources within several classrooms and collaboratively creates a lesson plan to address the chosen problem or question of practice.

3.  The group reflects on the evidence gathered and determines next steps based on the discoveries made, which occurs over an extended period.

Lesson study provides teachers with an opportunity to discuss and gain insight into the content that they are called on to teach, ways students tend to understand and approach the content that they study in school, and pedagogical knowledge and skills. Although each lesson study cycle focuses on just one lesson, the process enables teachers to reflect broadly on what constitutes good practice. By engaging in lesson study, teachers develop their skill in lesson design, highlighting the complexities of teaching while also considering together how best to address these complexities (Fernandez & Yoshida, 2004).

Lesson study takes a substantial amount of time and is not designed for rapid change. Evidence of change is not focused solely on pedagogy or curriculum but extends to ways in which teachers view teaching, learning, and their role in supporting student learning. Lesson study works best in mature and stable schools. Although it can include teachers with less experience, it requires a core of highly professional, motivated, experienced teachers (Stephens, 2011). Lesson study stands as an aspirational goal in which teachers truly function as a team, designing, implementing, and reflecting on learning experiences collaboratively.

### A Principal's and Department Chair's Experience with Lesson Study: Amy's and Jonathan's Story

When we last met Amy, we were witnessing a fundamental transition in her school. Comfortable with visiting one another's classrooms, at ease with multiple educational leaders in addition to Amy, and gaining respect for the voices and perspectives of all, Amy's faculty members are taking greater ownership of their professional learning. The story of professional learning in Amy's school can no longer be referred to as "Amy's story." Although it can still be written as "Amy's and Jonathan's story," we anticipate that soon even that will not be possible. The school is on the verge of a breakthrough to becoming a high-functioning team. Teachers are looking more frequently to their instructional rounds facilitators and even to one another

*Continued*

to reflect on their practice. The faculty room is abuzz not with complaints but with energized conversation about teaching and learning.

After several years of success with instructional rounds, Jonathan learned about lesson study and felt ready, along with his colleagues in the math department, to take on this practice of collaborative professional learning. During their scheduled weekly meeting, the math department teachers choose a lesson to create together that incorporates not only math skills—in this case, understanding very large numbers—but also the school's core values of kindness and creativity.

The team develops a lesson focused on determining the approximate volume and weight of one million grains of rice. Incorporating creative problem solving, the lesson can be adapted for students at all middle school math levels, including those in pre-algebra and algebra classes. With no clear formula dictating how to determine the volume and weight of one million grains of rice, students must engage in creative problem solving. The problem also engages students in considering the implications of their exercise for transporting food to hungry populations during natural disasters. The lesson in kindness hits close to home as well, as students work in collaborative groups where respect and empathy go a long way to facilitate problem solving.

The lesson study team members are excited to develop and expand their teaching, thinking beyond the exercises in their textbooks to activities that will be challenging, meaningful, and relevant. Jonathan models the lesson in his classroom first, with the rest of the department observing. The teachers then meet and identify components of the lesson that worked well and areas that can be improved. They revise the lesson to be taught by another teacher, making modifications based on their reflections and on the needs of students in this second classroom. After the teachers observe and critique the lesson a second time, they choose a new lesson to develop. This process continues in the math department throughout the year.

During the end-of-year schoolwide faculty meetings, the members of the math department share their lesson study experiences with the rest of the faculty, interesting other departments in engaging in lesson study as well. The faculty members also think about ways of incorporating conversations about lesson study into their cross-disciplinary instructional rounds networks.

Before Amy began visiting classrooms as a coach and implementing peer coaching and instructional rounds, lesson study would have been unimaginable in her school. Yet now it feels like a natural fit. Amy feels an overwhelming sense of satisfaction and pride: her school has evolved from a collection of individual professionals into a team.

## Conclusion

At the beginning of this chapter, we quoted Pasi Sahlberg on the importance of seeing teaching as a team sport rather than an individual race. The true impact of principal-coaching occurs once principals can turn their attention from coaching individuals to nurturing a team of professionals who have the maturity and skill to blend professional autonomy with a commitment to professional collaboration. It can be recognized when nonjudgmental feedback is being offered, reflective conversations are occurring, and collaborative planning is commonplace—not only between the principal-coach and individual teachers but also schoolwide. Getting to this place of creative collaboration and coordinated teamwork is time- and labor-intensive and occurs gradually, over the course of years. In our opinion, it is the single most powerful contribution to improving the quality of teaching and learning for our students, and it is the aspiration we set for all school leaders who truly seek to lead with a coach's hat.

## Put On Your Coach's Hat

*Reflect on your current reality:*

• In your school, is teaching seen as a team sport or an individual race? Do you have pockets of teams and pockets of individuals? Where in your staff do teams need to be nurtured?

• Who among your staff do you believe would be willing to step out of their comfort zones and pioneer teacher classroom visits in your school? Can you think of specific individuals, a grade level, or a department? Or could you start with your brand-new teachers?

• Are any of the classroom visit structures discussed in this chapter (peer coaching, instructional rounds, or lesson study) taking place in your building? If so, how have they influenced teacher learning and collaboration? If not, which one of these practices do you think could make a difference in teacher learning and collaboration in your building?

*Next steps:*

• Choose a structure that you would like to implement in your school. Reread the relevant section in this chapter and spend some time planning how this could look in your school.

• Talk to some of your trusted colleagues or teacher leaders to help build a solid plan before taking it to your staff.

—— Appendix ——

# Forms and Tools

The forms in this Appendix can be downloaded at http://www.ascd.org/ASCD/pdf/books/ CoachApproach2017forms.pdf. Use the password "CoachApproach117025" to unlock the PDF.

## Leadership Style Tracker

| Date | Name or Group | Time | Authoritative | Affiliative | Democratic | Coaching |
|------|---------------|------|---------------|-------------|------------|----------|
|      |               |      |               |             |            |          |
|      |               |      |               |             |            |          |
|      |               |      |               |             |            |          |
|      |               |      |               |             |            |          |

### Reflection Questions

1. What do you notice as you review the data?

2. Do you have a style that is more dominant than others?

3. Is there a style you use with specific groups or in certain situations?

4. How could one style lead to the use of another?

## Interactions Tracker

| Date | Name or Group | Time | Coaching | Management | Evaluative | Notes |
|------|---------------|------|----------|------------|------------|-------|
|      |               |      |          |            |            |       |
|      |               |      |          |            |            |       |
|      |               |      |          |            |            |       |

## Reflection Questions

1. What is your ratio of coaching to management to evaluative interactions?

2. What patterns do you notice? With specific teachers? At certain times?

3. What type of interaction is taking up most of your time?

4. Are there management or evaluative interactions that could shift to coaching interactions with a few minor adjustments?

# References

Allen, D. (2001). *Getting things done: The art of stress-free productivity*. New York: Viking Penguin.

Anderson, M. C. (2001). *Executive briefing: Case study on leadership coaching ROI*. Retrieved from http://www.findyourcoach.com/roi-study.php

Baeder, J. (2013). High intensity leadership [Webinar]. The Principal Center.

Baeder, J. (2010, October 17). What's a tickler file?! [Blog post]. *Eduleadership*. Retrieved from http://www.eduleadership.org/whats-a-tickler-file

Barkley, S. (2016, January 31). Exploring peer coaching [Blog post]. *Steve Barkley Ponders Out Loud*. Retrieved from http://barkleypd.com/blog/exploring-peer-coaching

Borysenko, J. Z. (2011). *Fried: Why you burn out and how to revive*. Carlsbad, CA: Hay House.

Boushey, G., & Moser, J. (2006). *The daily 5: Fostering literacy independence in the elementary grades*. Portland, ME: Stenhouse.

Boushey, G., & Moser, J. (2009). *The CAFE book: Engaging all students in daily literacy assessment and instruction*. Portland, ME: Stenhouse.

Burgess, D. (2012). *Teach like a pirate: Increase student engagement, boost your creativity, and transform your life as an educator*. San Diego, CA: Dave Burgess Consulting.

City, E. A. (2011, October). Learning from instructional rounds. *Educational Leadership, 69*(2), 36–41.

City, E. A., Elmore, R. F., Fiarman, S. E., & Teitel, L. (2009). *Instructional rounds in education: A network approach to improving teaching and learning*. Cambridge, MA: Harvard Education Press.

Covey, S. M. R. (2006). *The speed of trust: The one thing that changes everything*. New York: Free Press.

Covey, S. R. (1989). *Seven habits of highly effective people*. New York: Simon & Schuster.

Donaldson, G. A., Jr. (2007, September). What do teachers bring to leadership? *Educational Leadership, 65*(1), 26–29.

Drucker, P. (1967). *The effective executive: The definitive guide to getting the right things done.* New York: HarperCollins.

DuFour, R., & Mattos, M. (2013, April). How do principals really improve schools? *Educational Leadership, 70*(7), 34–40.

Fernandez, C., & Yoshida, M. (2004). *Lesson study: A Japanese approach to improving mathematics teaching and learning.* Mahwah, NJ: Erlbaum.

Foltos, L. (2013). *Peer coaching: Unlocking the power of collaboration.* Thousand Oaks, CA: Corwin.

Fullan, M. (2012). *Stratosphere: Integrating technology, pedagogy, and change knowledge.* Session presented at the ISTE Annual Conference and Exposition, San Diego, CA.

Gleeson, K. (2009). *The personal efficiency program: How to stop feeling overwhelmed and win back control of your work.* Hoboken, NJ: Wiley.

Goleman, D. (2000, March/April). Leadership that gets results. *Harvard Business Review.* Retrieved from http://www.deltacoach.com/Business_Coaching/PDF_files/ Entries/2008/9/16_Leadership_That_Gets_Results,_by_Daniel_Goleman_files/HBR%20 Leadership%20that%20gets%20results%20by%20D%20Goleman_1.pdf

Gordon, J. (2008). *The no complaining rule: Positive ways to deal with negativity at work.* Hoboken, NJ: Wiley.

Hall, P., Childs-Bowen, D., Cunningham-Morris, A., Pajardo, P., & Simeral, A. A. (2016). *The principal influence: A framework for developing leadership capacity in principals.* Alexandria, VA: ASCD.

Hattie, J. (2009). *Visible learning.* London: Routledge.

Hattie, J. (2012). *Visible learning for teachers.* London: Routledge.

Horsager, D. (2011). *The trust edge.* New York: Free Press.

Keller, G., & Papasan, J. (2012). *The ONE thing: The surprisingly simple truth behind extraordinary results.* Austin, TX: Bard Press.

Knight, J. (2007). *Instructional coaching: A partnership approach to improving instruction.* Thousand Oaks, CA: Corwin.

Knight, J. (2013). *High-impact instruction: A framework for great teaching.* Thousand Oaks, CA: Corwin.

Knight, J. (2011). *Unmistakable impact: A partnership approach to dramatically improving instruction.* Thousand Oaks, CA: Corwin.

Knowles, M. S., Holton, E. F., & Swanson, R. A. (2005). *The adult learner: The definitive classic in adult education and human resource development.* Amsterdam: Elsevier.

Losada, M., & Heaphy, H. (2004). The role of positivity and connectivity in the performance of business teams: A nonlinear dynamics model. *American Behavioral Scientist, 47*(6), 740–765.

Markow, D., Macia, L., & Lee, H. (2013, February). *The MetLife survey of the American teacher: Challenges for school leadership.* New York: MetLife. Retrieved from https://www.metlife. com/assets/cao/foundation/MetLife-Teacher-Survey-2012.pdf

Marshall, K. (2003). Recovering from HSPS (hyperactive superficial principal syndrome): A progress report. *Phi Delta Kappan, 84*(9), 701–709.

National Association of Secondary School Principals & National Association of Elementary School Principals. (2013). *Leadership matters: What the research says about the importance of principal leadership*. Reston, VA & Alexandria, VA: Authors. Retrieved from http://www.naesp.org/sites/default/files/LeadershipMatters.pdf

Nelson, J. (2001). *The art of focused conversation for schools: Over 100 ways to guide clear thinking and promote learning*. Gabriola Island, BC, Canada: New Society.

Palmer, P. J. (1998). *The courage to teach: Exploring the inner landscape of a teacher's life*. San Francisco: Jossey-Bass.

Rath, T., & Clifton, D. O. (2004). *How full is your bucket?* New York: Gallup Press.

Renwick, M. (2014). *Digital student portfolios: A whole school approach to connected learning and continuous assessment*. Virginia Beach, VA: Powerful Learning Press.

Robbins, P. (2015). *Peer coaching to enrich professional practice, school culture, and student learning*. Alexandria, VA: ASCD.

Robinson, V. M. J., Lloyd, C., & Rowe, K. J. (2008). The impact of educational leadership on student outcomes: An analysis of the differential effects of leadership types. *Education Administration Quarterly, 41*, 635–674.

Routman, R. (2014). *Read, write, lead: Breakthrough strategies for schoolwide literacy success*. Alexandria, VA: ASCD.

Sahlberg, P. (2015, October 5). Do teachers in Finland have more autonomy? [Blog post]. *The Conversation*. Retrieved from http://theconversation.com/do-teachers-in-finland-have-more-autonomy-48371

Stephens, M. (2011). Ensuring instruction changes: Evidence based teaching—How can lesson study inform coaching, instructional rounds and learning walks? *Journal of Science and Mathematics Education in Southeast Asia, 34*(1), 111–133.

Tracy, B. (n.d.). The law of forced efficiency [Blog post]. *Brian Tracy International*. Retrieved from http://www.briantracy.com/blog/business-success/the-law-of-forced-efficiency

Troen, V., & Boles, C. C. (2014). *The power of teacher rounds: A guide for facilitators, principals, and department chairs*. Thousand Oaks, CA: Corwin.

Tschannen-Moran, M. (2004). *Trust matters: Leadership for successful schools*. San Francisco: Jossey-Bass.

Tucker, R. (2008). *Leadership reconsidered: Becoming a person of influence*. Grand Rapids, MI: Baker Books.

University of Washington Human Resources. (n.d.). Professional coaching. Retrieved from http://www.washington.edu/admin/hr/pod/coaching

Urban, H. (2012). Keynote address presented at DART Regional Summer Teacher Academy, Mayville, WI.

Vander Ark, T. (2016, May 31). Visiting schools: Transformative professional learning [Blog post]. *Getting Smart.* Retrieved from http://www.gettingsmart.com/2016/05/transformative-professional-learning

Whitney, D., Trosten-Bloom, A., & Rader, K. (2010). *Appreciative team building.* New York: McGraw-Hill.

Wiggins, G. (2012, September). Seven keys to effective feedback. *Educational Leadership, 70*(1), 10–16.

# Index

Note: Page references followed by an italicized *f* indicate information contained in figures.

# About the Authors

 **Jessica Johnson** is the elementary school principal and district assessment coordinator for Dodgeland School District in Juneau, Wisconsin, and an adjunct professor in the Educational Leadership Department at Viterbo University. Named the 2014 Wisconsin Elementary School Principal of the Year, she has previously taught in Minnesota, where she earned her bachelor's degree at Bemidji State University, and taught and served as an instructional coach and assistant principal in Arizona, where she earned her master's degree at Arizona State University.

Jessica is the coauthor of *Breaking Out of Isolation: Becoming a Connected School Leader* (Corwin, 2015) and the author of a children's novel, *Adventures in Blockworld: A Novel for the Young Minecraft Fans* (2013). She co-moderates the #educoach chat on Twitter each Wednesday at 8:00 p.m. CST and cohosts the popular PrincipalPLN Podcast. She lives in Juneau with her husband and two sons, who keep her active coaching sports and robotics teams. You can follow Jessica on Twitter as @PrincipalJ or contact her at jessica@principalj.net.

**Dr. Shira Leibowitz** is founding lower school director of Portfolio, designed as a network of schools reimagining the possible in education through student-centered interdisciplinary project-based learning with academic, intellectual, and creative depth. Prior to joining Portfolio, Shira led independent schools in the greater New York City area for 20 years, serving as department head and curriculum coordinator, lower school principal, and head of school. She has coached teachers throughout the United States in implementing project-based learning and has led online communities of practice focused on educational innovation, teaching and learning, and instructional coaching. She is co-moderator of #educoach, a weekly Twitter chat focused on instructional coaching approaches.

Shira earned her bachelor's degree from Cornell University and her PhD in education from the Jewish Theological Seminary of America, including extensive study at Teachers College, Columbia University.

Shira lives with her husband Alfredo and is the proud mother of two children, Talia and Ronen. Also included in her family are two dogs, a cockapoo named Oliver and a Jack Russell terrier named Max. You can follow Shira on Twitter as @shiraleibowitz.

**Kathy Perret** is an educational consultant for Northwest Area Education Agency in Sioux City, Iowa, focusing on the areas of teacher leadership, literacy, and English as a second language, and an adjunct professor at Morningside College in Sioux City, Iowa. She has also been an instructional coach at the elementary and middle school levels and currently serves as an educational enhancer for her private consulting business, Kathy Perret Consulting, providing learning opportunities in the area of instructional coaching.

Prior to her consulting and coaching work, Kathy spent 18 years as an elementary teacher in Iowa, serving students at St. Rose of Lima in Denison, Woodbury Central Community School District in Moville, and Sioux

City Community Schools. Staying connected with her former students via social media and seeing their contributions to the world fill her with pride.

Kathy earned her bachelor's degree in elementary education at Iowa State University in Ames, Iowa; her master's degree at Morningside College in Sioux City, Iowa; and her Iowa PK–12 Administrative Endorsement through the Iowa Principal Leadership Program in Storm Lake, Iowa. Kathy also holds endorsements in the area of K–8 Reading and K–12 ESL.

Kathy enjoys spending her spare time as a community and state volunteer. She is currently the board secretary for the Mary Elizabeth Child Care Center and a volunteer with the Canine Assisted Therapy Program for STARS, Inc., both in Sioux City, Iowa. She is the former president of several organizations, including Leadership Siouxland, the Siouxland Reading Association, and Learning Forward Iowa.

Kathy is the proud aunt to three nephews and one niece and the guardian to a rescued Schnoodle named Boji. After much training and coaching, Boji became a certified therapy dog, and together Kathy and Boji bring joy to others through the K9 STARS Read-to-Me Program. You can follow Kathy on Twitter as @KathyPerret or contact her via http://kathyperret .net.